Simon Armitage was born in Huddersfield in 1963. After reading Geography at Portsmouth Polytechnic followed by a course in Social Work and Psychology at Manchester University, he worked for some time as a probation officer. He has won many prizes for his poetry, including one of the first Forward Poetry Prizes in 1992 and the *Sunday Times* Young Writer of the Year award in 1993, and in 1994 he received a major Lannan Award. Now a freelance writer and broadcaster, he has written extensively for radio and television, and continues to live in West Yorkshire.

Glyn Maxwell was born in 1962 in Welwyn Garden City, and read English at Oxford. In 1987 he went to Boston University to study poetry and playwriting with Derek Walcott. His three collections of poetry have won various awards, including the Somerset Maugham Travel Prize in 1992. He has written several plays and a novel, which was shortlisted for the Whitbread First Novel Prize of 1994. He teaches creative writing at the University of Warwick.

MOON COUNTRY

Further Reports from Iceland

SIMON ARMITAGE
and
GLYN MAXWELL

faber and faber
LONDON · BOSTON

First published in 1996
by Faber and Faber Limited
3 Queen Square London WC1N 3AU

Photoset by Wilmaset Ltd, Wirral
Printed in Great Britain by
Mackays of Chatham PLC, Chatham, Kent

Simon Armitage and Glyn Maxwell are hereby identified as
authors of this work in accordance with Section 77 of the Copyright,
Designs and Patents Act 1988

A CIP record for this book
is available from the British Library

ISBN 0-571-17539-2

2 4 6 8 10 9 7 5 3 1

Contents

Moon Country

Iceland

Midnight. Vodka, down
in one. Spied through the bottom
of the bottle: sun.

Scotch on the rocks, straight
down. Seen through the empty glass
the moon. It's twelve noon.

Assurance

Where water hurtles down so long an age,
Assure yourself what Father took for rage
Is calm, is almost sleep here, where the earth
Would make a mountain of its mildest birth.

Assure yourself that moments down the lane
This same water patches the charred plain
With comic pools, po-faced to no avail,
That purse and bulge, then let like a sperm whale.

And where there's fire a year, for a thousand years
There's this its lumpy memory that smears
The valley like a curse but, like a story,
Reddens the passing mind to the passed fury.

Where there is air like Arthur breathed, there's steam
Up from a subterranean oxen-team,
And near where the ice is slit like a sniper's eye,
Stalagmites of it, marvellous, metres high.

No story ends, no man-commanded rocks
Bar the intriguing cave to the bone that knocks:
All ends are strewn like places to start out,
Assured of nothing, armed with unageing doubt.

TO WHOM IT MAY CONCERN

Glyn Maxwell and Simon Armitage, Freelance Presenters
working on behalf of the British Broadcasting Corporation, will
be travelling to Iceland between 25th August and 11th
September 1994, and I hereby authorise them to carry
recording equipment consisting of:

(1) 1 DAT PDK20
     Serial Number 120627

(2) 1 SONY D7 Kit No. 1
     Serial Number 44998

Could you please afford them all the appropriate help
necessary for them to carry out their duties.

I confirm that the equipment is necessary for them to record
material to be included in programmes to be transmitted on
BBC Radio, and I further confirm that the equipment is *not* for
resale and will be returned to the UK after use.

DATED: 24th AUGUST 1994

Kit Bag

Personal

1 pair Line 7 blue/grey 'Light-trek' Gortex walking boots; 1 pair dark-brown three-hole ankle-length Doctor Martens: both size 9. 12 pairs M&S black cotton-rich socks; 12 pairs assorted M&S undies, boxer shorts & briefs; 1 pkt travel-size washing powder (biological). 3 × black Levi's 615s, 1 two-inch leather belt with silver buckle, 1 pair blue Troll leggings to double as long-johns. 5 × white + 5 × black XL Banana Republic 100% heavy cotton T-shirts, 4 × assorted button-down check shirts, Bronx Clothing, Huddersfield. 1 plain black all-occasion lightweight jacket, 1 hurricane-proof zip-up anorak with detachable hood.

Sony Walkman WM-FX43 plus Boots HE-6 in-ear headphones plus Sony SRS-18 mini-speaker system plus 12 Ever-Ready Energizer 1.5v alkaline batteries. 200ml silver hip flask plus contents. 35mm 1:4 Olympus Trip MD plus 12 rolls Kodak Tri-x film. Silver/gold Parker 8mm roller-ball pen plus refill. Boots 'Notebook' series A4 & A6 hardback notebooks. 18-function Swiss army knife. Book of matches, length of string. 1 Slazenger tennis ball. *National Geographic, NME, TLS, Letters from Iceland.*

Naked – Talking Heads. *Boy Child* – Scott Walker. *Debut* – Bjork. *Hatful of Hollow* – The Smiths. *The Infotainment Scan* – The Fall. *Swoon* – Prefab Sprout. *Blonde on Blonde/Bringing It All Back Home/Bootleg Series* – Dylan. *Document* – R.E.M. *Absolute Classic Masterpieces* – Felt. *Doolittle* – The Pixies. *It's a Shame about Ray* – The Lemonheads. Selected slim volumes – nothing over 50pp p/b and/or 3oz.

Gillette Cool Wave shaving gel with advanced lubricants for unsurpassed razor glide; pkt 10 Gillette Blue II Plus with

Lubrastrip. Sure Super-Dry anti-perspirant deodorant for men; Kouros Tonique Après Rasage 1.6 fl. oz. atomiser. 1 × 100ml tube Mentadent P with fluoride; Mentadent 'Diagonal' toothbrush, red and white. 75mg indomethacin slow-release capsules, one to be taken nightly or after food; 1 pkt Crooke's Sea-Legs as approved by St John's Ambulance; pkt ten Lemsip sachets, original flavour; 1 btl. approx. 100 paracetamol (contents may settle during transit). Sainsbury's Lipsave lip balm, 1 stick; 1 tube 'quickactin'' Tinactin athlete's foot cream. Denman 5″ hairbrush with nylon bristles; Alberto VO5 Power hair gel, for mega hold and total control.

E.C. passport. Documentation and ticketing. BBC statement of intent and declaration of property, Icelandic Tourist Board 'waiver' in Icelandic, 30-page itinerary plus notes and required reading. Credit cards, Eurocheques, cash and assorted ullage.

Perpetual Almanac of Saints and Folklore Diary.

Technical

Big black tape-recorder. Little blue tape-recorder. Microphone with fun-fur cover. Microphone with sticky bit on back. Black and red wires. Tapes. Batteries plus charger (labelled 'Batteries' and 'Charger'). Instruction manuals × 5.

St Bartholomew's Day

After sharpening his crampons, topping up his hip flask with something warm and smooth and salvaging his woollen jumpers from the assorted bedding in the dog basket, Mr Petersson left a scribbled note on the mantelpiece, posted the latchkey back through the letter-box and stumbled down the unmetalled track, his three holdalls swinging like a bolas. The hire car was a Ford in pearlescent green, automatic, and he gunned the throttle, sending the needle well into the red, then, after finally engaging a suitable gear, pulled off along the velvet roads of West Yorkshire towards the motorway. At every change of pace his left foot fished for the slow plunge of the clutch, and his right foot found the huge brake pedal with such ease and effect that at one point he almost executed a servo-assisted triple salko with pike through the windscreen. Not that this stopped him attempting to break the sound barrier at every available opportunity, the inclination being to thrash the bollocks off any piece of equipment belonging to a corporation or company, and in anticipation of sitting behind the steering wheel in a foreign country he was reminded of the joke about the English Siamese twins, joined at the hip, who went abroad because the other one wanted to drive.

The M1, Britain's main artery, was clogged and clotted at several points along the journey, as was the London Orbital, which he entered like a steel ball into a roulette wheel, fingers crossed, hoping to fetch up in the slot market 'Heathrow'. After winning that particular lottery he made five complete circuits of the airport in search of the hire-car drop-off point, and at one stage considered leaving the vehicle on the central reservation with its engine running and the hazard-warning lights flashing, hoping the police might dispose of it in a controlled explosion. When he had finally deposited it at the appropriate place he was

8

conveyed on a glorified golf buggy to the correct terminal, where he met with Mr Jamesson, who arrived encumbered with a bewildering assortment of shopping bags, rucksacks, briefcases and bin liners, each with its own deficiency such as a split seam, a broken clasp, a sprained buckle or a snagged zip. Items of a personal nature erupted from every opening, marking his passage through the concourse, and upon noticing this Mr Jamesson retraced his steps, stuffing handfuls of socks and underthings into his jacket pockets. A pair of red boxer shorts went the way of all things, becoming legged up in the wheel of a luggage trolley and disappearing around the corner, past the Bureau de Change.

A whistle-stop tour of the duty-free area and a quick calculation regarding the legal importation of alcoholic refreshment into Icelandic airspace resulted in the optimum purchase of wines and spirits, and upon hearing their names called for the last time over the public address system they sped along the moving walkways like a groom and a best man late for a wedding, and were given an old-fashioned look by the air hostess as she bolted the aeroplane door behind them.

Having being allocated a seat that was neither aisle nor window, Petersson contented himself during a faultless flight with the *National Geographic* (stinger-box jellyfish off the coast of Northern Australia and an identity parade of ten-year-olds from downwind of the Chernobyl district, all offering the same deformity to the camera, all smiling) and a pair of ill-fitting in-flight headphones, available for the price of two non-returnable pounds sterling and with a capacity for transmitting both music and headache. Jamesson on the other hand made the most of the view, and gave a running commentary of the plane's position based on the street patterns of Britain's major conurbations and the floodlights of stadia known to be hosting first-class football fixtures that evening. Both travellers incorporated three or else four small bottles of wine into their personal itinerary, and another two or three more into their hand luggage.

At the two-hour mark, it was noticed that the aircraft was heading continuously towards a hazy and uncertain brightness that seemed to hang in a semicircle over their destination, a dome of green-grey light, silvery even at its edges, as if the moon were lying in wait at the far end of the flight path, the moon face up in the water, or a land giving back the shine of the moon. But they descended into black fog with thick rain shearing across the windows, and touched down diagonally, causing the tyres to squeal and the captain to apologise, and when the chief steward announced the temperature and weather conditions outside the cabin it occurred to Petersson that he was back in the Pennines.

Being glass and wood like a modern church but more welcoming and functional, the airport was also spotlessly clean and had the additional attraction of an actual-size single-seater flying machine suspended from its ceiling. Neither Mr Petersson nor Mr Jamesson was searched or even questioned by the uniformed staff, which was fortunate on the one hand but on the other hand led them to wonder if they shouldn't have concealed more contraband liquids about their persons. In the end, they concluded they were right in not destabilising the fragile Icelandic economy (based on alcohol tax if the stories of beer at ten pounds a pint were to be believed), and went clinking into the cool air towards the car park.

Keflavík airport, they observed from outside, was no bigger than a modest multi-screen cinema complex on a trading estate on the outskirts of a provincial English town, though certainly easier to exit, and the two of them were driven at a safe speed towards the capital and their first overnight accommodation. En route, they witnessed the colour-coded system-built hangars and barracks of the American military, looking very much like Moon Base Alpha or some other extra-planetary settlement. A search-light with a green eye threshed a three-hundred-and-sixty degree arc across the premises, illuminating housing blocks and more sinister installations.

After the suburbs, a bridge that might have been a flyover and a couple of glimpses of the ocean, they were deposited at the Hotel Loftleiðer in the middle of the night, agreeing with each other that *the land of the midnight sun* was a figure of speech rather than an actual scientific phenomenon – something that they might be grateful for, suggested Jamesson, being this close to the ozone hole. After the formalities of checking in and a lucky escape in the paternoster lift, Petersson retold the one about the Icelandic boy making his way upstairs towards the bathroom and his mother shouting after him 'And don't use all the cold water.' He then retired to his room, drew the thick, heavy curtains which could only have been designed with an air-raid in mind, and burrowed down inside the complicated layers of sheets, coverlets and duvets. Ten minutes later he found himself torn between the Gideon Bible to his left and the mini bar to his right, but he thought better of both and fell into a deep sleep accompanied by appropriately deep dreams.

St Louis' Day

At breakfast, Petersson tried out his first words of Icelandic on a man who turned out to be a weights and measures expert from Oldham, Lancs, flown in the previous evening to recalibrate a church clock. Venturing outside, he found himself drawn to a domed building on a nearby hilltop, a fancy restaurant with a revolving roof, offering a circular view of the capital, and from that position the angular and colourful architecture gave the impression of a neat and tidy Lego-land, assembled only recently. Across the bay, the mountains looked as if they had risen from the sea that very morning, and the sky was a blue ocean without so much as a ripple of cloud.

Upon Jamesson's timely appearance, the two of them made their way to the bus depot and scrambled onto a waiting coach for a guided tour of the city. Over the tannoy system, the guide trotted out a number of facts and figures, some more memorable than others. Jamesson made a note that Iceland experienced two murders every three years, and that most university departments were financed through a national lottery. Also, that the population of the country is in the region of a quarter of a million, with 150,000 living in the capital, and Reykjavík roughly translates as 'Smoky Bay', though there is probably less smoke here than anywhere else in the developed world. The bus passed across a stretch of open grassland where a man was exercising his dog by throwing it out of the car window and driving away at full speed, then through an area known as Snob Hill, where house prices were in the region of telephone numbers, including the full international dialling code. A nursery with a dozen or so blond-haired infants within its perimeter fence had the look of a scene from *The Village of the Damned*, but this thought went unspoken as the bus pulled up outside the Museum of Art.

The building appeared to resemble an igloo or an albino turtle, consisting internally of a lobby or hall connected to a hollow white shell or cupola, entered via a spiral staircase, and its acoustics reminded Petersson that one of his grandfather's many claims to fame was that he had once broken wind in the Whispering Gallery of St Paul's Cathedral. True to the spirit of the age, the main space was dominated by an exhibition of manhole covers from around the world, and the two visitors were circumspect in their examination of the museum's other acquisitions for fear of finding themselves admiring a radiator or a power-point.

The tour then proceeded to an enormous church, Hallgrímskírkja, the tallest thing by far on Reykjavík's skyline, christened after Iceland's most beloved poet and inspired, architecturally speaking, by mountains and ice caps. Inside, they signed the visitors' book with their proper names, but Petersson was lying when he reported overhearing a conversation between two American tourists, along the lines of 'D'ya think this is Lutheran, Wanda?' – 'No, hon, it's probably mahogany.' By far the most striking feature of the church, both men agreed, was the grand organ with its four manuals, seventy-two stops, mechanical tracture and 5,725 pipes, like the exhaust system of a vehicle capable of annihilating the land-speed record. Back on the bus, the tour guide rounded things off by reminding everyone that this was Friday night, that Friday night in Reykjavík was more drunken and chaotic than anywhere else in the northern hemisphere, and that God-fearing and upright citizens should make their way back to the safety and comfort of their hotel. Being largely agnostic and morally horizontal, Mr Petersson and Mr Jamesson salvaged their very swankiest shirts from the bottom of their suitcases, complete with give-away folds across the chest and stomach like the tropics of Capricorn and Cancer, and set off into the early evening. By 4 a.m., the midnight sun still hadn't risen through the windows of whichever bar or café they were slumped in, so they called it a day, crawled into the back seat of a taxi and were very kindly delivered like two pints of milk to the doorstep of their lodgings.

Harald and the Lonely Hearts

An Icelandic Entertainment

PROLOGUE

Twelve Beermats from Café List

Down the first one. Hosted, Happy,
Independent, Noting, New.

Mine's the second. Scornful, Snappy,
Cool, Comradely, Arch, Askew.

You get this one. Rare, Reflective,
Owed, Opinionated, Sure.

Yours? No, mine. Serene, Subjective,
Dreamy, Daring, Insecure.

Mine now? Maybe. Halve it. Honest,
Hot, Incautious, Merry. Men.

Chasers, nice one. Young, Unpromised,
Promised, Precious. Really? When?

Is this one local? Silent, Serious,
Photogenic, Pheline, Low.

This one's better. Dim, Delirious,
Ill, Illumined, All-Aglow.

Better spend it. Licked, Unloving,
Ugly, Surly, Skint, Aghast.

Shouldn't maybe. Blithe, Believing,
Cold, Confessing, Cracked, Recast.

Afore we go. Direct, Decided,
Pure, Pedantic, Puzzled, Pale.

Us in Iceland. Happy, Hosted,
Quaff the Fucker. Tell A Tale.

ACT I

(*Café List, Reykjavík, in the small hours between Friday and
Saturday. The* BARMANSDÓTTIR *serves the last customer,*
HARALD.)

BARMANSDÓTTIR

Drink up, Harald, drink it down,
You're the only one so it's only fair,
Get out there, Harald, out on the town
With the youth of the nation the worse for wear.

HARALD

I don't mind that, oh they'll wait for me,
They'll be there for hours, all wondering what
Old Harald's up to – I'm up till three!

BARMANSDÓTTIR

Three?

HARALD

Three-thirty, as like as not.
They love me, don't they, I'm good-time Hal,
The thousand picking-and-choosing girls,
They spell my name on the Höfði wall,
And a dozen beribboned and ice-white curls
Spring as they glance at –

16

BARMANSDÓTTIR
That silhouette.
Him and his silhouette, all night long.

HARALD
You have to admit how it's nobly set,
The nose and the lips and the chin so strong,
Everyone says so, they can't all be wrong.

BARMANSDÓTTIR
Not everyone says so (and drink that down
For I'm closing up). You should change your song.
There's someone who eyes you under a frown.

HARALD
My brother, you mean. Well there's a surprise.
I too would be jealous if I had a conk
Like one of our horses, and horse-fly eyes
Like Hoskuld has! All day I'd be drunk!

BARMANSDÓTTIR
So no change there. Get out on the street,
You bane of all women, you cock of the north,
There are lampposts to lie to, gutters to greet,
It's Friday in Reykjavík, stumble forth!

HARALD
The fun can begin, now I'm on my way!
Our Nordic Dark has annulled the Day!
I'll wait till it's almost blue in the air,
Then leap to the street and be loved down there!
I'll wait till the light is a breath from the sky –
How I'll shock my girl as I hear her sigh!

Song of the Lonely Hearts Standing
around Reykjavík

(Sung by KARINA, MAGNUS *and their million friends)*

The bars are all closed and the clubs are too full
A million of us have been to school
A million of us could not care less
That the clubs are too full and the streets are a mess!

The streets have been sick on themselves, so what?
A million of us can take a shot
Of our million drinks in our million bags
Now the bars are all closed and we've had our fags.

There's nowhere to go in our capital town!
It's here or it's bedtime, it's here hands down!
We'll talk about chat about stuff about talk
By the light of the moon and the songs of Björk.

We came here for love and we're still hanging out
With the sons in a sulk and the dottirs in doubt
But a million hearts can patter together
And nobody needs to go home with another.

Call us the lonely hearts, call us the boozers,
Call us the louts and the liggers and losers,
Here's where we stand in the well of the dark
Singing Up with the lot of us, down with the lark!

The clubs are all closed and the firmament fills
With the glinting of stars by the glowering hills
But a million of us will stop where we sway
When the stars hear the seagulls and call it a day.

We'll never do that, we'll shine in the shade,
Not alone or in love or asleep or afraid,

Unready for dreaming, strangers to beds,
While Saturday's swirling about our heads!

Off with it, out with it, Friday for ever!
Staggering back with our shoulders together,
Back to sobriety, school, and then
It's a rapid U-turn and we'll start up again!

What do we want with our million minds?
Oblivion when the thin sun shines!
Indifference when the noonday drums!
And more of the same when the twilight comes!

Call us the lonely hearts, call us the boozers,
Call us the louts and the liggers and losers,
Here's where we stand in the well of the dark
Singing Up with the lot of us, down with the lark!

(HOSKULD *walks by, in thought.*)

MAGNUS
Hey Hoskuld, what you done with your brother?
We missed him tonight and the morning's near.

HOSKULD
Who knows? Am I his keeper, his mother?
Don't worry about him. I've had an idea.

INGE
Oi, Hoskuld, where's Harald?

HOSKULD
Been doing some thinking . . .

MAGNUS
Just like his brother!

KARINA
Hoskuld, dear,
Where's handsome Harald?

HOSKULD
I didn't say *drinking*!

KARINA
We're missing him badly!

HOSKULD
You want my idea?
I said I'd been *thinking* – didn't you hear me?
I've got an idea, a suggestion, a notion.

INGE
What's Horseface saying? (Don't you come near me)
There's comelier folk in the Arctic Ocean.

HOSKULD
Look at you all, a million swiggers,
Lacing the street like the salt on the sea,
Look at yourselves, you must all feel as sick as
The English Navy in '73.
But let me be Throstur and lead you a dance now,
The sick and the lonely, the low and the scruffy,
All of you follow me on the advance now,
Home to my flat for a mug of coffee!

(*The* LONELY HEARTS *of Reykjavík fall silent and stare at*
HOSKULD.)

MAGNUS
He's got to be joking. We never do that.

INGE
He can't fit a million into his flat!

HOSKULD

So what there's a million, we'll all squash up.
Room for ten thousand on every shelf.
Say a hundred thousand to every cup
And it's damn good coffee, I brewed it myself.

MAGNUS

But that would mean nobody standing here!

KARINA

Teeth never chattering, nobody ill!

INGE

No one regurgitating his beer!

MAGNUS

It'll never catch on, oh it never will.
What would become of our reputation,
Youngsters of Reykjavík, Friday's flowers,
What would become of the ancient tradition
Of freezing our rocks off in the small hours?
No, no, I say. Horseface is jealous,
There's the truth of it. Let's keep swaying.
Hours to go.

INGE

    Meanwhile, won't you tell us
Where Harald has got to?

KARINA (to Magnus and Inge)

You may be staying,
But I want to try out his coffee idea.

INGE

But Harald, Karina, shouldn't you wait for him,
Isn't he going to ask you out?

21

KARINA

He's stood me up, and now it's too late for him.
Me, well I'm weary of standing about,
Till a certain somebody deigns to appear.

KRISTJAN

Me too, this is silly, this outdoor palaver.

HERMANN

Yeah, I'm with Horseface, it's boring here.

GUDRUN

Like waiting for snowdrops to sprout in the lava!

KRISTJAN

Like waiting for cuts in the price of beer!

HERMANN

Horseface's flat where we don't mind the squash!

GUDRUN

Horseface's flat where we're going to be snug!

KRISTJAN

Horseface's flat for a wee and a wash!

KARINA

Three cheers for coffee and good old Horsemug!

(*The* LONELY HEARTS *of Reykjavík follow* HOSKULD *towards his home.* MAGNUS *and* INGE *are alone. They realise how cold it is.*)

MAGNUS

Too bad for Harald, he should have been early.

INGE

Hardly our fault if he's missed his turn.

We'd better run after the hurly-burly.

He's lost his place now. He'll never learn.

Secret Walking Song of Hoskuld

No one knows it
No one visits
So no one knows it
Where is it, where is it?
Where lives Horseface?
Where kips the beast?
Where will he brew for us
Beans for a feast?
Far place, flat place
Some steps east.

No one loves me
No one enquires
For no one loves me
The blind and the liars
Where lies Horseface?
Where does he shout?
Where does he beat for us
Skins for a rout?
Far place, flat place
X miles out.

No one knows it
No one visits
So no one knows it
Where is it, where is it?

Where strides Horseface?
What has he planned?
What does he clench
In a bone-white hand?
What are we up to,
What follows *and*?

> *Far place, flat place*
> *Yards inland.*
> *Far place, flat place*
> *Yards inland . . .*

Fresh Walking Song of the Lonely Hearts

Call us the lonely hearts, call us the boozers,
Call us the louts and the liggers and losers,
Now we are walking, we all have a date,
We've coffee to drink and we mustn't be late!
We've coffee to drink and we mustn't be late!
We've coffee to drink and we mustn't be late . . .

(*The* LONELY HEARTS *vanish from Reykjavík.*)
(HARALD *leaps out to surprise them, and is surprised to discover*
that they are not there.)

HARALD

Pinch me, punch me, wish me the winter,
Paddle me north in a vest and socks,
On a Friday night in Reykjavík Centre
The streets are abandoned for blocks and blocks!
Karina, Karina! Kristjan, Hermann,
All of my friends, have you left me alone?
Has somebody howled you a horrible sermon,
Has somebody threatened you over the phone?
What is the point of a beautiful figure

With no one to stand side on and admire?
Did you shrink, did I grow, did the world get bigger?
Am I for ever to play Town Crier?

(The disconsolate HARALD *sees in the distance the monstrous silhouettes of* FOUR TROLLS *walking up Laugavegur towards him. The* LARGEST TROLL *comes forward and grins.)*

TROLL

Lonesome, innit? Ain't it only?
Loveless, is it? Or only lonely?

HARALD

I'm sure there's a reasonable reason for it.

TROLL

Right, like it's maybe the season for it.
Everyone gone, no fun, no fun.
Fancy a nightcap? We'll give you one.

HARALD

But nothing's open.

TROLL

By my twin dicks,
Café Trunt Trunt opens up at six.

HARALD

Is that where they've gone to?

TROLL

By my one ball,
They're gone, and we're off. Accept it, that's all.
Tag along, we ain't got Saturday jobs.

HARALD *(sotto voce)*

I'm not that surprised, if you've got two knobs.

(*The* TROLLS *bring* HARALD *to Café Trunt Trunt. The* HAPPY
COUPLES *are sitting in pairs and staring at each other in silence.
The* LARGEST TROLL *introduces himself as* GLOTA, *and his fellow
trolls as* SHRUGGA, STURRA *and* DROPPA.)
(GLOTA *buys a round.*)

GLOTA

Have a beer, boys.

SHRUGGA

Whatever, whatever.

GLOTA

Have a beer, boys.

STURRA

Glota, you never
Buy any rounds. You've something in mind.
Don't trust him, my man, he's not your kind . . .

GLOTA

Have a beer, boys.

DROPPA

Don't mind if I do.
The Editor of *Morganblaðið*, he drinks this too.
I said to him only this week –

GLOTA

Hush your noise.
We've come here to cheer up Harald, my boys.
Skald!

TROLLS

Skald!

HARALD

Don't mind if I do.
Who says I need cheering up?

GLOTA

Don't you?
Not that I'm one to gloat, you know,
But I heard of a place where you'd like to go,
There's singing and dancing and fun and frolics,
It's brilliant there!

STURRA

If you like alcoholics.

GLOTA

Hush up! The point is, we don't know where.
But we do know it's Hoskuld who took them there.

HARALD

Hoskuld my brother? But he's my mate!

SHRUGGA

Tough shit, get another.

STURRA

You're much too late.

DROPPA

Looks like your social life went down the tubes,
But I'll put you in touch with the Sugar Cubes.

HARALD

Where did he take them?

GLOTA

Home through the snow.

27

HARALD

Where does he live then?

GLOTA

Shouldn't you know?

HARALD

We drifted apart.

GLOTA

Well they drifted his way.

HARALD

Where can I find them?

GLOTA

Yesterday.

HARALD

It just isn't fair. They've left me behind
All alone in the town without friends or dates!

STURRA

That's not very nice.

SHRUGGA

Can't say I mind.

DROPPA

I might tell Vigdís.

GLOTA

We'll be your mates!

HARALD

I don't need your help. You can't even see
How handsome I am. But it's jolly well clear
You're ugly as sin and you gloat over me,
And I hate you, I hate you. I want more beer.

GLOTA

Beer you shall have. But Café Trunt Trunt
Is full of good people, or didn't you notice?

HARALD

No, they're so quiet.

GLOTA

So why don't you hunt
For some new friends here, if you don't like gloaters?

HARALD

I'll do just that. I'll get a new crowd.
So long as they're humanoid. I'm not proud.
Anyone want a drink with me?
Anyone want to share a view?
Anyone want to partly agree?
Anyone want what's new? What's new?

(HARALD *tries to make friends at the tables.*)

Chorus of Happy Couples

Ignore him and he'll go away.
Ignore him, he'll leave town.
Ignore him and we'll pass the day
The same way that we passed the day
The other day. Eyes down.

Eyes down, he'll move a world away.
Eyes down, he'll emigrate
Eyes down and then we'll pass the day
The same way that we passed the day
The other day. You wait.

29

For I have you and you have you,
    We share you happily,
And both of us will pass the day
The same way that we passed the day
    The other day. With me.

Forget him like a memory.
    Forget him like a sky.
Forget him and we'll pass the day
The same way that we passed the day
    The other day. He'll die.

(*Café Trunt Trunt empties, but for* HARALD *and* GLOTA *the troll.*)

HARALD

So every Lonely Heart has gone
From Reykjavík, and all who stayed
Have settled for the only one
They have?

GLOTA

You've cracked it, I'm afraid.

HARALD

And all who love or look for love
Have wandered somewhere no one knows
With brother Hoskuld – heavens above!
Why him?

GLOTA

Charisma, I suppose.

HARALD

What can I do?

GLOTA

Why, do your best.

HARALD

But what is best?

GLOTA

Why, look inside
The heart in an Icelandic breast
And let the island be your guide.
When and whatever you decide,
Let the island be your guide.
And now I'm off.

HARALD

But is that all?

GLOTA

I have a date, by my one ball.

HARALD

But can't I have some clues or tricks?

GLOTA

'Twin sisters, by my double dicks.

HARALD

No magic to imagine by?

GLOTA

Three villages, by my third eye.

HARALD

No help at all, no love to spare?

GLOTA

It's Saturday. So long. So there.

(GLOTA *is gone.* HARALD *goes to bed. And sleeps.*)

Top Secret Dance of the Coffee Lovers

Hush! Cool! It's Hoskuld's Kingdom!
Drink it dark
Or drink it creamy
Dance! Sweat! It's Hoskuld's Party!
Dance it slick
Or dance it dreamy
Creep! Step! It's Hoskuld's Business!
Watch him close
Or watch him only
Flop! Sleep! It's Hoskuld's Chamber!
Never lost
Now never lonely

Friday 26th August

'Harvest by now well advanced: make strengthening pottage for harvest workers'

Lunchtime when they emerged, unshaven and unbreakfasted, and made their way to the Marine Research Institute, where Jóhann Sigurjónsson was waiting with Danish pastries and black, bituminous coffee. On a computer screen in the corner of his office, the three of them followed the progress of an electronically tagged fin-whale, zigzagging across the North Atlantic. The Director explained that a country completely dependent on the sea for its economy doesn't take kindly to the superpowers issuing their Thou Shalt Not commandments from on high – and it mightn't be long before the fleet starts sharpening its harpoons again. There was long and heavy silence, brought diplomatically to an end by Mr Petersson, who was grateful on behalf of the whale on the screen that the only thing stuck in its flesh for the time being was a transmitting device and a long-life battery. Mr Jamesson was at one moment tempted to reach for the cursor control and guide the creature into calmer waters, and wondered out loud if the tag itself might end up as a speciality dish in a Japanese restaurant.

The Fault at Thingvellir

Nothing did this. It's not a wound or weal.
It's just two bodies passing. It's really a dance
under a swaddled sun and this fan of steel
so fast it makes you cold. This is a glance
in time, a glare of likeness between two
tagged *Europe* and *America*, like calling
stars after the farm animals we knew.
This is the future rearing, it befalling.

It isn't even Iceland. This is under.
Like giving bones your name, you wouldn't, would you?
This rumbles by, unusable as thunder,
this long and helpless hauling of the land
across itself.
           You couldn't bear it, could you?
Stick out a hand or flower like this hand.

St Monica's Day

The drive to Thingvellir, site of the world's oldest parliament, was a two-hour journey between high and narrow valleys, and through the windscreen of the car the image was that of a fibre-optic camera making its way down the oesophageal tract, or a voyage through computer-generated fractals. Icelandic horses ran alongside the car, demonstrating their peculiar gait – a sort of fifth gear somewhere between a canter and a trot – the way horses ran before the invention of the moving picture. More interesting than the ancient seat of government was the fissure in which it sat, a trench caused by the tectonic plates of Europe and North America pulling away from each other at so many centimetres per year. Making their way to the head of the gorge, Petersson asked Jamesson how it had been for him, and Jamesson replied that the earth had moved. After exchanging metaphors based on the separation of the two continents, they parted company and for thirty minutes threw insults and stones at each other across the divide.

Another hour in the car brought them to Gullfoss waterfall, where the icy mud from two glaciers tumbles between two basalt precipices in the shape of the Hvitá river. Momentarily overtaken by the spirit of adventure and the notion that this was an expedition rather than an experience, they scrambled out to the most dangerous point for the sake of a photograph, and returned ten minutes later soaked to the skin and wondering what had come over them.

The almost eponymous geysers at Geysir were on good form on the day of their visit, with one particular blow-hole unable to contain itself for more than a couple of minutes, and the old proverb of a watched pot never boiling was disproved time and time again, as the two travellers peered into the seething well of

35

foam and steam, then ran for cover with the water beginning its own drum-roll somewhere underground. The notion of a 'natural phenomenon' was called into question at this point, in as much as a hole in the ground retching plumes of super-heated water at regular intervals was probably the most unnatural thing in the world. The guidebook had warned them that Great Geysir, the grand old daddy of the Geysir family, is now impotent and at rest, and can only be persuaded to spout every now and again by the addition of fifty kilos of soap, thus reducing surface tension down in its bowels. Petersson flicked an extra-strong mint into blue, sleepy waters, but as a laxative this proved insufficient.

To every side were smaller, more comical geysers, all of them bubbling with amazing colours, one gurgling like a saucepan of molten chocolate, another like custard, with a smaller pool of tie-dye purple just inches away from it. It was almost as if a Turner Prize-winning artist had been at the site only ten minutes before tipping coloured powders into the holes to make a metaphorical point about an artist and his/her palette or a reflexive pun on the term 'landscape painting'.

That evening, they wandered into town and parked themselves at the bar in the Café List. Towards the end of the night, Petersson realised that he had been agreeing for at least two hours about the greatness of Auden, whereas the man he was talking to was actually speaking about Odin. Evidently there was very little to distinguish them.

Matthías Johannessen

Poet, Editor of Iceland's Daily Paper *Morganbla*ðið

'Auden was a very likeable man. At once, when you met him, he was so friendly. What I remember best was when we were sitting down with the poets . . . Auden stood up there, thanking us for the reception, and in his speech he said – and this moved us Icelanders – that he was visiting holy earth. And this I never forget, because he meant it. [He had] said that Iceland was like the sun that had set, [but] you could see the sunshine on the mountains: Iceland followed him like that – the colours of the setting sun on the mountains. He said he was not always thinking about Iceland, but . . . that he was never *not* thinking about Iceland.

'What he liked the least was the noise from the radio, in the buses, in the cafés, he told me he just hated it. I couldn't do anything about it. All of a sudden I wanted to be a dictator . . . I would have stopped the radio for the hours and days he was here.

'Dust settles; poetry must not settle. So we do it both ways, we use everything if we want to. When you get a piano you don't use only five [notes], you use the whole scale, don't you? You want to play everything which comes from here, like a bird – he's not thinking *I'm going to sing like that, I'm going to sing like that*! The tree doesn't mind. The bird is there and he sings how he wants to sing, not how he should sing, because the tree is a very good listener.

'When I was a young newspaperman there was an old man – I had published two of my books of poetry, or something like that – I was talking to him, I loved to have interviews with old people, with common people, with seamen, people who have been there and there, and who have been carrying all these tales in all kinds of forms in their heads . . . I said I wanted to talk to him and he looked at me and he said "Me? No, you see you cannot understand me, because between me and you there are one thousand years. I am a contemporary of Egil Skala-Grímsson but you are a modern man."

'And I am longing for these people, to meet them. They are gradually vanishing. Also, they had this wonderful clang in their language, they spoke beautiful language, which is not as good as it was. But I must admit that we had some Danish influence at the time, in the last century, so it was good to get rid of that. We don't use foreign words if we can. We use foreign words only for a year or two years, and all of a sudden there comes a *thoghta*, a jet. *Simi* is a telephone. They used the Danish or international word *telephone* for several years but they never liked it. It stuck to them as lice. They had to get rid of these foreign lice – like the salmon who comes into the rivers – it takes them two days to get rid of the international lice in the ocean! So gradually they are liceless in the Icelandic rivers! These people . . . stopped talking about *telephone*. When I was young, people said to me as a child "Get me the telephone!" Nobody says that today. It is *simi*. It comes from threat, it's an old Viking word for threat.'

Two Fools at Gullfoss

No one to stop us coming here. No one
to guide us, steer us, sting us, blare a proverb,
curse or motto into the blistering creature,
        water's commando, scorner of fat oceans.

No one to tell us how, where from, what for,
no one to help us, save us time, or save us,
should we be about to do the thing we did do,
drop,
        two boneheads dared to a precipice,
and kid about one another's being one another's
Literary Executors. Meaning

*hey, we could die at Gullfoss, we could gently
go from here, be borne in the crushing silence,
no? we could die at Gullfoss.*
                        If we have done,
perhaps they have got around to an oblong sign,
say, splashed out on a booth with a bloke thumbing
Nordic Wives while practising his warning
against the water, against getting near that water,
because, do you know the facts about that water?

That wouldn't stop us. Nothing ever stops us.
Nothing ever stops us.

¶

From where we stand
bananas and vines
do well

on account
of the hell
underground.

Springs and the like
are marked on the map
under smoke,

the greatest of geysers
washes its mouth
with soap.

A glacier strays from the range,
grazes the plain
at its own sweet pace,

snouts
for a sense of itself
at the lip of the lake.

St Augustine's Day

Brilliant sunshine. Most of the morning was spent trying to find yesterday's football results and cricket scores on the car radio, but the closest they came was to locate the voice of Perry Como, being played on American Forces Network for Lieutenant James Donnelly, on his birthday, with love from wife Barbie and all the kids. Happy birthday, Jim. After sprucing themselves up, Mr Jamesson and Mr Petersson walked to the Bummannsklukkan Restaurant for the 'poets' lunch', where they were seated opposite each other at a circular table in the company of some of Iceland's leading literary figures. The guest list read as follows: lecturer Ornulfur Thorssen; Halldór Guðmundsson, Editorial Director of publishing house Mál og menning; Sveimbjörn I Baldvinsson, poet, teacher, and head of RUV TV; author Steinunn Sigurdardóttir; novelist and Chairman of the Writers' Union Einar Kárason; and poets Linda Vilhjálmsdóttir, þrarinn Eldjárn, Sjón, and Bragi Ólafsson – Bragi being one-time bassist with the Sugar Cubes but having traded his electric guitar for a fountain pen.

Sjón stood up and recited two poems in Icelandic, and the two Englishmen applauded, which was just as well because the poems turned out to be translations of their own work. Petersson recalled that a line in one of his poems, 'kipped for an hour in the cash-point lobby', was once translated into Macedonian as 'smoked fish for sixty minutes in the wage demonstration', and Jamesson was quick to admire the improvement. Appropriately enough, the story was told of Auden's line 'Every poet has a name for the sea' becoming 'Every port has a name for the sea' because of a printing error, and Auden's preference for the mistake over the original. Much wine was glugged. Einar Kárason informed the party that the manager of the restaurant had a fearsome reputation, and on one occasion had sunk his teeth into Einar himself during an altercation. When Petersson asked 'Where did he bite you?', Einar replied 'Behind the dustbins', and another bottle of red was ordered.

Spilling out onto the street they were surrounded by crowds of people twirling black and white scarves above their heads, and cars were nose to tail along Reykjavík's main street, sounding their horns and displaying pennants and flags of the same colour. In the Icelandic equivalent of the FA Cup, Reykjavík had just overcome a farmstead on the north coast by two goals to nil, and whilst this didn't strike the two English poets as a momentous achievement, the majority of the population of the capital seemed gripped by a strange mixture of jubilation and relief. Not wanting to break with the spirit of things they followed their hosts to the nearest bar for a celebratory drink, or two.

The session was captured on camera by Petersson, who is to be seen in the background of his own photograph courtesy of a mirror, with his hands in front of his head and a huge flash of white light for a face, as if performing some strange act of primitive magic, one that has made all the other people in the photograph smile. Jamesson, astonished and with red eyes like the devil's, is hiding behind what must be at least a quart of lager.

Before the end of the evening, two points were made on the subject of language. Firstly, according to the Icelanders, Norwegians sound like drunken Swedes trying to talk to their babies. Secondly, the word for a person who speaks two languages is 'bilingual', and the word for the person who speaks only one is 'English'. There was no offence meant, and none taken.

Trunt

According to the tale of 'Trunt, Trunt, and the Trolls in the Fells', a man out picking Iceland lichen (for its edible fronds) is captured and carried off by one such troll woman. After three years, he appears before his friends, now in the form of a horrible troll. He no longer believes in God, but in 'trunt, trunt, and the trolls in the fells'.

Iceland, from Past to Present, Esbjörn Rosenblað and
Rakel Sigurdardóttir-Rosenblað

It's here, it's now, it's nowhere else,
Trunt, trunt, and the trolls in the fells
It's Glyn, it's getting it if God wills,
Trunt, trunt, in a mood in the hills
It's right by the window, close as a star,
Trunt, trunt, in a fight in a car
I'm very much for it. It's what I'm for.
Trunt, trunt, and the trolls at the door . . .

It's easy, it's well-nigh impossible too,
Trunt, trunt, and the trolls at the zoo
It's never been done and it's never been new,
Trunt, trunt, and a trap come true
It takes only seconds but they have no ends,
Trunt, trunt, and the tops off pens
It picks without pity the time it spends,
Trunt, trunt, and the trolls have friends . . .

I know what it's not, only not what it is,
Trunt, trunt, and the trolls at a quiz
It's never to come and it's not what you miss,
Trunt, trunt, on a coach in a kiss,

43

It's all that I feel minus all I know,
  Trunt, trunt, and a snog in the snow
I'm taking it with me the night I go,
  Trunt, trunt, and the trolls say 'You go . . .

It's not what you think of the show so far,
  Trunt, trunt, and the trolls at the bar
It's making a meal of the meat you are,
  Trunt, trunt, in a jam in a jar
It's all that I wanted, it's all I got,
  Trunt, trunt, in a coat in a cot
It's mine and I'm having it and that's your lot,
  Trunt, trunt, and don't ask me what.

Monday – The Commemoration of the Beheading of St John the Baptist

Bank Holiday (UK except in Scotland)

At the University of Reykjavík, Dr Pál Einarsson unlocked the door of a tiny office, inside which two dozen seismographs were ticking and twitching, each one hooked up to fault-line or volcano, reporting the slightest movement in the Earth's crust. Dr Einarsson confirmed what Petersson and Jamesson had already worked out for themselves, namely that Iceland is one of the world's valves, a sort of cork or bung, or a wound in the Earth's skin that keeps mending and cracking, mending and cracking as the planet flexes its muscles. Petersson tried to take the metaphor a stage further by suggesting that Iceland is the belly-button of the world, the location that connects the inner with the outer, a symbol of birth and renewal, but upon receiving no support from his colleague he changed tack and asked about the influence of the landscape on the outlook of those who attempt to inhabit it.

Talking personally rather than professionally, Dr Einarsson suggested that it was impossible not to be affected by the sight of a mountain rising from the ground in front of your eyes, or by the prospect of opening the bedroom curtains each morning and looking out on a different horizon. Even as they spoke, four or five of the seismographs relating to the north of the country began to fidget, and finally the needle on one of the machines scribbled a frantic pattern across its roll of graph paper, like a child going mad with a crayon. Seismographs take the pulse of the land, check its heartbeat, Dr Einarsson explained, and what they were witnessing that day was not a cardiac arrest exactly, but certainly a murmur or a palpitation.

Being close by and with a couple of hours to kill, the two men wandered across the campus to the Árni Magnússon Institute,

45

home of the world-famous Saga manuscripts, kept under lock and key and controlled atmospheric conditions. The building was officially closed, undergoing essential earthquake-proofing, and draped in scaffolding and orange plastic webbing looked more like one of Christo's early efforts than a repository for literature's very own Ark of the Covenant. Nevertheless, in what can only be thought of as estuary Icelandic Mr Jamesson managed to convince the security officer that here were two poets eager to pay homage rather than a couple of tourists wanting to take snapshots, and they were duly invited to sign the visitors' book. A quick search for the signatures of Auden and MacNeice proved unsuccessful, mainly because the book went back no further than April of 1994.

They were then met by the most senior curator, Mr Stefán Carlson, a Father Christmas-like character who very kindly led them down the corkscrew of a set of spiral stairs and into the basement, where one of the manuscripts was pinned open under glass, like a prehistoric butterfly. It turned out to be part of the story of Eric the Red on his voyage across the Atlantic, and Mr Carlson, after checking the nationality of his two visitors, couldn't resist quoting Oscar Wilde, pointing out that the Icelanders had been clever enough to discover America five centuries before Columbus, and also intelligent enough to forget about it. Following his finger across the lines of red and black ink was like watching Merlin poring over a book of potions.

Mr Carlson informed the two of them that many of the Sagas were written on the hides of sucking-calves, which looked in their preserved state something like unleavened bread, or the wafer-thin pancakes served in Chinese restaurants, usually with shredded duck. Feeling privileged and not a little smug at having managed to wangle their way into the vaults for a private viewing of Iceland's crown jewels, they then waited for the green light on the time-lock to replace the red one, and walked tall through the metal-detector and out into the sunshine.

On the assumption that the gods must be on their side that day, they thought they might try their luck at the White House, site of the summit meeting between Presidents Gorbachev and Reagan in 1986. The house itself was a white clapboard affair in the centre of a small strip of lawn on the shoreline, and could easily have been mistaken for a sailing club or a weather station. After knocking on three of the doors, they were eventually admitted by a man in a red cardigan, clutching his head and sipping from a glass of Alka-Seltzer, a man who kept insisting that a permit must be obtained to see the house at the same time as he apologised for the mess and ushered them into the front room. Two minutes later they were back out on the stoop, reflecting on their whirlwind guided tour and trying to recall some of the details, such as the pot plant on the copper coffee-table, the photograph of the two world leaders on the wall and the surprising lack of fortifications or security devices. It was difficult to believe that ten years ago America and Russia had been discussing the end of the human race in a shotgun shack on Reykjavík prom, surrounded by fixtures and fittings more in keeping with a mid-sixties semi-detached than an international conference facility. But what was more puzzling was that the house should now be occupied by a man with a hangover, and it was fair to presume that both the weather system of cigarette smoke and alcohol fumes still circulating above the picture rail and the wine bottles erupting from a plastic bin-bag outside the kitchen door were not unconnected to his condition.

At the Department of Corrections, neither Mr Jón Sigurdsson nor Mr Erlendur Baldursson would confirm the rumour that Icelandic prisoners were allowed to retrieve the football if it was kicked over the fence during a match. Having spent some time as a probation officer in a former life, Petersson expressed a wish to visit the local jail, where he was met by a large man in a spotted

47

bow-tie, drinking from a bottle of pop and sucking on a long length of bootlace liquorice, who felt the need to address Petersson in the voice of Kenneth Williams and made constant references to Radio 4 comedy programmes of the seventies and eighties. Petersson was reminded of the scene in *One Flew Over the Cuckoo's Nest*, where the inmates of the asylum with their various mannerisms, idiosyncrasies and twitches are introduced to a suspicious official as doctors and professors, and get away with it. It also confirmed to him that prisons, whatever their purpose, are universally unpleasant and always smell of boiled cabbage. As he left, the heavy wooden door slammed shut behind him, and Kenneth Williams was saying 'Toodle pip' through the hatch, turning the key in the lock at the same time.

In the evening, an interview with top Icelandic footballer Gudni Bergsson (Tottenham Hotspur, but none the less a very fine player) had to be cancelled because of his call-up for international duty against Sweden later in the week. It left the two poets kicking their heels at the training ground, watching seven- and eight-year-old girls practising free-kicks and showing the sort of ball control that would have shamed at least half the current England team. After leering through the mesh fence for about half an hour in genuine admiration, they skedaddled to the bar just as some concerned parents were beginning to get the wrong idea.

Soccer Players at Valur

Their grounds, with two main grounds and two practice
    pitches,
Were loud and bright with a fair sprinkling of players
When we got there in our car with some sketchy questions.
They were all already out there being teams,
Already having tottered up on the concrete
High up on eight studs each, wanting the turn of soft grass,
Now out there playing important parts in big striped teams,
Having those sudden diagonal tempers of thought
Useless in class but worth a try out there though,
Even to end in the low relief of a foul,
Or the twenty-two man hug of a fine shot saved.

And here we came, imagining they were watching,
Stopping to see us clomping sunnily out
Of the clubhouse now: here come the English Headphone
    People,
The Generals – all goodwill and good intentions . . .
To tape the air and chat across it crisply,
Rap with an existentially interested-bored goalkeeper,
Or with some heavy, heaving, substituted striker
We last saw plus a beer maybe, or the Captain if we found
    him,
Get him to run through the highs and lows of the '93–4
    season,
And then when we'd finished, even (I know I hoped so)
Strip off at the laughed suggestion, play for some minutes,
Tape it, *the poets!* board the First Division
Of Iceland, dine out drunk on the thing in London!

We were glad with this in our thoughts as we got nearer,
But equally so to let it lower to the green
Evening grass, gently, then sit down to watch these matches, these
Girls' games, Icelandic girls playing excellent soccer
Oblivious to our testing of our sound levels
By their main grounds and their suddenly shimmering
    practice pitches.

¶

From where we stand
the land
unzippers itself

and frets,
and a proverb exists
on the setting

of cups and plates
too close
to the table edge.

The sun is a coin
on the loose,
spiralling down

around the Arctic rim;
the days
are strained and sieved

through the nights,
and the nights arrive
with the days stirred in.

Tuesday

'Candy roses while they still bloom: beware heat-sleepy adders.'

After sprucing himself up in readiness for the event that night, he was met by Jamesson in the hotel lobby, and a game plan was hatched in the back of the taxi which conveyed them to the Café Sólon Íslandus, venue for an evening of English and Icelandic poetry. As it turned out, everything went according to plan, and as was usual on such occasions the two men charged each other with the task of speaking an unrelated word or phrase at some point in the reading. Petersson got himself out of a seemingly impossible snooker by mentioning 'textured vegetable protein' while introducing a poem about the Last Supper, but Jamesson went one better when he made 'isosceles triangle' the concluding rhyme in a Petrarchan sonnet. They were outdrunk and outdressed by their Icelandic counterparts, and to sidestep the thorny philosophical issue of poetry in translation, the two of them read entirely in English. At the end of a very successful evening they were joined by three military men of indeterminate rank from the American Air Base at Keflavík, attending the reading as the obvious alternative to either the in-house basketball quarter-final replay (Motor-pool v. Flight Staff) or another night at Idaho Joe's Honest Injun Steak 'n' Bake Place.

Harald and the Lonely Hearts

ACT II

A week later. Café Sólon Íslandus. A poetry reading is just ending.

POET
Here's how they rated him when they looked back.
Sometimes he did this. Sometimes he did that.

(Applause. HARALD *walks in with a fat volume and takes the stage.)*

HARALD
Excuse me, sir, but it's my turn now.

PETERSSON
You're not on the bill. Is he with you, Max?

JAMESSON
Vaguely remember him, don't know how.
Too freaky for Faber. Too pretty for Bloodaxe.

HARALD
But look, I've composed a modern-day Edda!

PETERSSON
Show it to Horovitz.

JAMESSON
Into the shredder.

HARALD
And a brand new million-part Icelandic Saga!

PETERSSON
Melt him a medal.

JAMESSON
Loan him a lager.

HARALD
I was told to search in the breast of the land
For the answer to where all my friends have gone!
I know what to do! I understand!
An Edda! A Saga!

JAMESSON
A loony.

PETERSSON
Not wrong.
Who told you all this?

HARALD
Why a troll, of course!

PETERSSON
Max, are you certain he's not one of yours?

JAMESSON
If he's one of your dogs then he's slipped your leash.

PETERSSON
Come on. I could murder that guillemot quiche.

(HARALD *begins to recite his Saga.*)

HARALD

sky scary with skeletons	rotten rain rushing
wolf walks wrathfully	boats bob bitterly
twas twelve score hours	since spirits desported
trees tussle tittering	Harald howls horribly

(*The* POETS *and their* AUDIENCE *leave the café.* HARALD *finds himself alone. A large glass of beer materialises before him. As he lifts it, the light catches it and, as he lowers it,* GLOTA *appears opposite.*)

HARALD

Lies, you old troll. Who wants a poem?
They all want dancing and sex and noise.
I'll do it, I'll find 'em and then I'll show 'em,
Those cosy old couples and poetry boys.

GLOTA

Better look deeper then, deeper than song,
And better go faster, you can't hang about,
I'm not one to gloat, but you've not got long:
Rumour is, Hoskuld is sorting them out!

HARALD

What can you mean?

GLOTA

Why the beautiful girls,
He's making them coffee, he's making them pine,
The doll and the darling, the strawberry-curls,
The minx and the moll and the maid –

HARALD

That's mine!
Karina, you say! She was waiting for me,
Waiting all night in the pitying cold,
She went with my brother, my sworn enemy?
He's making her coffee?

GLOTA

Of a blend of gold,
Though I'm not one to gloat. Follow me, friend,
Deep into Iceland, deeper than song.

HARALD

Damn you, Karina! Drinking Gold Blend
With that son-of-my-mother! It's wrong, all wrong!

(GLOTA *leads* HARALD *through a door, whereupon he loses his balance and falls down. He finds he is on a fishing trawler in a raging storm. The boat is crewed by* SHRUGGA, STURRA *and* DROPPA.)

Dead Stoical Sea Shanty

STURRA
Yo ho ho.

SHRUGGA
Bottle of Rum.

STURRA
Boat's gonna go.

DROPPA
Better swig some.

STURRA
Yo ho hay.

SHRUGGA
Bottle of Bell's.

STURRA
Judgement Day.

DROPPA
Hence those smells.

STURRA
Yo ho heg.

SHRUGGA
Bottle of Jack.

STURRA
All gonna peg.

DROPPA

Came for the craic.

STURRA

Yo ho hoem.

SHRUGGA

Bottle of Gordon's.

STURRA

Better read a funeral poem.

DROPPA

Not sodding Auden's.

STURRA

Yo ho hickhead.

SHRUGGA

Bottle of Vermouth.

STURRA

Harald is a dickhead.

DROPPA

Ain't that the truth.

STURRA

Attention all ships.

SHRUGGA

Bottle of Vod.

STURRA

Harald's gonna have his chips.

DROPPA

Better fish for cod.

HARALD

That's enough one-liners, you skeleton crew!
I'm going to be a fisherman, and gravad-lax to you!
I'll do as my forefathers, I'll farm the raging sea,
I'll feed the island, clothe the children, then you'll see!

(*The storm subsides.* HARALD *is fishing alone on a calm ocean. Suddenly he notices a tiny rowing-boat moving rapidly in his direction. He sees in the boat two pale, thin, ghastly creatures. It is the* NIGHTMARE ECO-MODEL *and her brother the* GREEN CHILD.)

Green Maritime Dissuasion Song

MODEL

Pull up your net, cut off your line,
Go hide, go home, go hungry.

CHILD

Leave everything in the sea alone,
Be off, be gone, I'm angry.

MODEL

You can't fish here, you can't fish there,
Go hide, go home, go hungry.

CHILD

You can't fish frigging anywhere,
Be off, be gone, I'm angry.

HARALD

But what about our children? How
Can anyone eat, miss?

MODEL

Our consciences do not allow
Us to allow you this.

HARALD

But what about our livelihood,
Our heritage, our waters?

CHILD

I don't accept it's for your good,
Nor do my seven daughters.

MODEL

I've friends, you know, in Hollywood,
Go hide, go home, go hungry.

CHILD

Caucasians bad, Cetaceans good,
Be off, be gone, I'm angry.

MODEL

We'll do a gig, we'll do a shoot,
Go hide, go home, go hungry.

CHILD

The strong will kneel before the cute,
Be off, be gone, I'm angry.

(HARALD's *trawler is escorted back to Iceland by a flotilla of the combined navies of Geneva, Los Angeles, Milan and Crouch End. He goes to Café List for a drink and a sealburger. The sealburger grows flippers and becomes* A REAL SEAL.)

HARALD

Overfished my quota, Glota.

GLOTA

How'd you penetrate my disguise?

HARALD

Don't fool me an iota, Glota.
You're fibbers all so damn your eyes.

59

I'll never see my friends and never
Soothe the girl whom I adored!
I'm all alone with you for ever.
You're yawning, Glota. Are you bored?

GLOTA

We haven't finished, nowhere near,
You ought to save your breath like me,
It may be hours before it's clear
To you what's coming, mon ami.

HARALD

I've written sagas, fished the oceans,
Done the work of Iceland folks,
Knot me nooses, pour me potions,
Tell me ten Norwegian jokes.
It's Hoskuld's story, I'm his zero,
I'm some sub-plot fall-guy stooge.
Couldn't you find a better hero,
Someone pretty, wise or huge?
Are you about to let *him* hog a plot here?
Rather than President Finnbogadóttir?

GLOTA

Far, and farther, deeper, deep,
Where the Westmen writhe in sleep,
Where the Vikings cast their throne
Upon a landmass so alone:
How to live where animals
Had never crept, and hissing hells
Were all that fumed across the cinders:
How to spend the spiting winters?
But here's a vision, here's a shock,
Torn out of the *Landnámabók*,

A country wooded from the peaks
And green through slopes and plains and creeks,
Behold the Past –

HARALD

Excuse me, troll,
Don't oversalt your minor role,
Turn into snacks and seals and beer,
But don't wash up a balladeer,
It's wearing wafer-thin, your charm.
And Hal's ripe for the funny – FARM!

(GLOTA *the seal vanishes, and* HARALD *finds himself alone, inland, grazing cattle.*)

HARALD

Where are you, Glota? Haven't I won?
Have I not delved the past enough?
I'm Hal the Good Icelandic Son.
I'm Farmer Hal, it's land I love.
I've made a bleak but homely place,
An outpost for the world of men,
A watch-tower for the human race!
Can I not see my friends again?

(*A sharp wind whistles across Iceland, carrying a tune.*)

Secret Lament of Karina

Whenever is my turn?
Whenever is my turn?
Someone says I'm next in line
For Hoskuld's coffee urn!

Whenever will it stop?
Whenever will it stop?

Someone halt the dancing please
For I'm about to drop!

Wherever are my friends?
Wherever are my friends?
Someone flick the pages quick
And fax me how it ends!

(The wind drops and the song fades.)

HARALD
Must have dreamed it. Never mind.
I know what's next for me.
For I'm not wanted in this land.
I'll sail immediately.
I'll sail immediately.
For I'm not wanted in this land.
Must have dreamed it. Never mind.
I know what's next for me.

(HARALD sets off wearily towards Reykjavík harbour. The CATTLE resolve themselves back into the FOUR TROLLS.)

STURRA
Let's follow him and take the mick.

SHRUGGA
Don't care. Whatever's fine.

DROPPA
It's all been an atrocious trick.
It's great!

GLOTA
I know! It's mine.

(HARALD reaches the deserted harbour. There are no more ships sailing out of Reykjavík, because only the Lonely Hearts know how to sail. The

HAPPY COUPLES *are all in their homes, playing Trivial Pursuit, and Iceland has ceased to be a trading nation.*)

Chorus of Happy Couples (*reprise*)

History, now that's my bag.
History, that's yellow.
With History we'll play the game
The same way that we played the game
The day before tomorrow.

Literature, that's more my scene.
Literature, that's brown.
With Literature we'll play the game
The same way that we played the game
That autumn in our town.

Roll after me, my lovely one,
Pursue me to the moon.
And chase me round it as you did
The day you did and when you did
Don't end my afternoon.

Nature, that's me out of it.
Oh Nature, oh that's green.
With Nature we have played the game
The same way that we'll play the game
When none of this has been.

(HARALD *walks sadly to the water's edge, and contemplates the end.*)

HARALD

Of all the lonely hearts there are
There's always only one about.
The luckiest of wishful stars
Is always on the voyage out.

The most miraculous of cures
Can only help if happened on.
Of all the rocks the heart endures
It founders on the furthest one.

(*He prepares to dive into the deep.*)

HARALD

If I'm a fall-guy I'd better fall.
God Bless Iceland!

GLOTA

Did someone call?

(GLOTA, *in the shape of a vast puffin, catches* HARALD *in mid-air, then flies high over Reykjavík with him, and sets him down atop the Pearl Restaurant.*)

GLOTA

What are you playing at, Handsome Hal?

HARALD

Handsome? that's really amusing, pal.

GLOTA

You seem to be throwing the towel in rather.

HARALD

Are you my brother? Are you my father?
Leave me alone like everyone does.
You and your chums.

GLOTA

Well don't blame us.
It's you Icelanders who filled each cave
With us, we were happy in Hell –

HARALD

Behave.

I'll jump from here.

GLOTA

There's a lovely view.
You can see quite far to the east, can't you?

HARALD

Thanks for the tip. I'll count the summits,
Or, more exciting, watch for comets.

GLOTA

You see that glow, not many miles hence?
You'd keep it in mind if you had any sense.

HARALD

If *you* had any sense, you'd change this venue.
The puffins round here all belong on the menu.

GLOTA

If you want to see your girl again, strike out for the ridge
Before the Northern Lights appear, stand up on the edge!
I'm not supposed to have told you this.
But it seems I have. Goodnight. God Bless.

(GLOTA *vanishes.* HARALD *sees a smoky fireglow emanating from the plain of Thingvellir, out to the east. He hears the tune again.*)

Secret Lament of Karina (*reprise*)

> *Whenever is my turn?*
> *Whenever is my turn?*
> *Someone says I'm next in line*
> *For Hoskuld's coffee urn!*

Have you seen the Lights?
Have you seen the Lights?
Someone says they'll flutter round us
One of these grim nights!

The curtain and the crown!
The curtain and the crown!
Then we'll hurtle till we halt
In our beloved town!

Volcanova

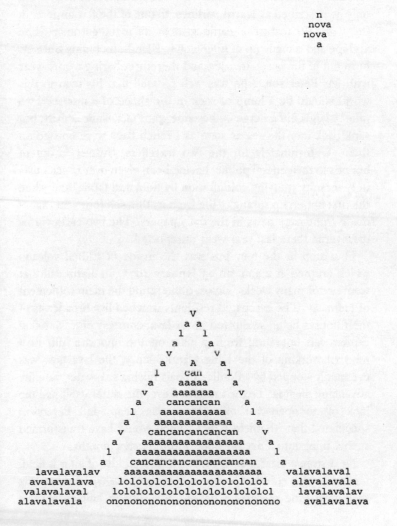

St Aiden's Day

By light aircraft to the Westman Isles, as customers of what could only be described as Icarus Airlines, to one of the few airports in the world to feature a cattle grid at its main entrance. The archipelago is made up of fifteen or so islands, including Surtsey, born out of the ocean in 1963 and therefore sharing a birth-year with Mr Petersson, who was well pleased that his twin in this world should be a lump of rock in the shape of a mouse. Two other islands did emerge in the same spurt of seismic activity, but sank back into the sea as soon as French flags were hoisted on them. Unfortunately for the two travellers, Surtsey is out of bounds to the general public, having been given over to scientists in spacesuits studying colonisation by flora and fauna, and when the first buttercup sprang to life from its thin soil four years ago it made front-page news in the daily papers. The two earthworms discovered there last year went unreported.

First stop in the tour bus was the inside of Eldfell volcano which erupted at 2 a.m. on 23 January 1973, an alarm call that went on for many weeks, almost obliterating the main settlement of Heimaey. The evacuated residents watched live broadcasts of their houses being swallowed up by lava, courtesy of a television camera left operating from a mast on the opposite hill. In a modern working of the King Canute story, the lava flow was eventually stopped by a flotilla of boats hosing sea-water onto the advancing magma. To the untrained eye, the crater itself had the look of an open-cast mine or a slag heap, and Petersson speculated that Sheffield City Council would have transformed such a thing into a dry ski slope within twelve months.

Next stop, a bizarre rock garden in the middle of an ash field, tended by two elderly *Gardeners' Question Time* types cultivating their own little piece of Chalfont St Giles in half an acre of

68

hell. From there, the coach made its way to the cliff tops and the tour guide produced a large box from under the back seat, containing at least two dozen puffin chicks. She explained that the juvenile puffins are often reluctant to fly, and to give Mother Nature a helping hand the good people of the islands round up the stray birds, point them in the direction of the sea and hurl them into the air. Petersson selected a bird from the box, and, cupping it gently in his hand, strolled purposefully over to the cliff edge and tossed it into the warm thermals rising from the water, only to see it plunge fifty feet without even flapping its wings and come to an abrupt halt on the rocks below. Not to be put off by the stunned silence of other tourists and the sobbing of their children, he recruited yet another chick from the batch and this time threw it higher and further, hoping it might catch the breeze and break into flight. This time the bird twirled downwards like a seed-propeller or a disabled helicopter, then nose-dived into the ocean, leaving two or three bubbles and a handful of feathers at its point of entry. Ten minutes later the bird still hadn't surfaced, and Petersson returned to the bus, sitting right at the back, well away from the whispers and withering looks of the other passengers.

The tour concluded on a small cruiser, eventually sailing into a large green cave, where the guide and his mate took out a trumpet and flute and struck up a version of 'My Way', with the tune bouncing back and forth against the walls of the cave, in time to the slap of water against the side of the boat.

In the evening, Mr Jamesson and Mr Petersson were the only customers for the seven o'clock showing of two films at Heimaey Theatre, one on the eruption of 1973 (highlight, a tractor ploughing ash from the roof of the hospital) and the other the re-enactment of one man's epic tale of survival after being thrown overboard three miles out to sea into freezing water. The leading role was played by the survivor himself, thus requiring him to walk once again over razor-sharp lava in bare feet, and bob up and down in a heavy swell close to treacherous rocks. Both features looked as though they might have been filmed on Sellotape considering the amount of hair and fluff that passed across the projector, but were sufficiently real to put the fear of God into both men in anticipation of their expedition on a trawler the next day. The voyage had been in some doubt up until the arrival at their hotel of Mr Hilmar Rosmundsson, an old man of the sea who pointed at the number six on his watch, jabbed Mr Jamesson in the chest and said 'You will be there.' Jamesson took this to be an instruction, rather than a suggestion.

For supper, Mr Jamesson ordered the catch of the day – breast of blackbird in a raspberry sauce, which he considered a variant on the usual four-and-twenty baked in a pie. However, the bird in question turned out to be a mistranslated guillemot, and tasted of liver.

Log of the *Gullborg*, 1 September 1994

or, 'The Water Is Not Very Still'

You will be there.

Every appointment dreaded, every school to have to go to, every lesson unprepared, every job to hate to do. Old Mr Rosmundsson is walking purposefully across the Westman Isles and they're not big isles and he has the power to summon. Old white-bearded Mr Rosmundsson is arriving at the Hótel Bræðraborg on the last day of August 1994. Old white-bearded, grave-eyed Mr Rosmundsson is seeking out the man he is sure to find. The sky is turning nasty and the weather is about to change. It is the middle of the afternoon, just gone. The sea has been calm for weeks.

Maybe we can just interview them maybe.

The man is in half-sleep in his hotel room, stirring uncomfortably, sighing over the low volume of his MTV, contemplating his mini-bar, thinking of ways of getting out of everything. He is half asleep in Heimaey, on the Westman Isles, off the south coast of Iceland. His friend is in a room down the corridor, watching CNN, but his friend is not the man upon whose door, loudly, three times –

You are BBC. You are Harmitage. You are Moxwell.

Well you know, we've been thinking (and it's true that we had, us, Petersson and I, been thinking about maybe in view of time constraints not actually *sailing* with the fishermen maybe *talking* with them, interviewing them) you know, we've been thinking –

You come, tomorrow, six o'clock, to the dock.

Jamesson is barefoot in the lobby of the Hótel Bræðraborg. He says he needs his producer. She'll tell you, we have to get back to

Reykjavík, have a talk to the President, need our strength, need our, well, maybe a chat with the men and then –

You will be there.

Every appointment dreaded, every school to have to go to, every lesson unprepared, every job to hate to do. Breakfast is at five a.m., mouldy ham sandwiches in the basement of the hotel. School day. Did not want to get out of bed. Was frightened of the old man. Wanted to go home. Three anoraks each, gallows humour. Lucky T-shirt, thing worn in the summer, in the garden, then, there, with them, those days. Black coffee, tastes of *must, have to, can't get out of.* Jamesson: I have maritime ancestors, I wonder if they'll help me. Petersson: I live as far from the sea as an Englishman possibly could live. Jamesson: do you think there'll be a bar on the ship? Petersson mummifies himself with anti-seasickness tape. Jokes are told in two ways, thickly and thinly.

I have maritime ancestors.

> As down the western welkin rode
> Day's cloud-illuminating god,
> And, bathed in his all-gilding ray,
> The valleys green and mountains grey
> Smiled farewell to departing day,
> And welcomed the autumnal eve,
> Of Scotland Maxwell took his leave.

Being the opening of William Billington's 'The Pilot Maxwell', written in 1883 and published in a Blackburn anthology: *Lancashire Songs, with other poems and sketches.* The Pilot Maxwell's name was James. He was my great-great-great-grandfather, a ferry pilot off western Scotland in the 1820s, at the perilous dawn of the paddle steamer. My name is Jamessonssonssonssonsson and I'm a poet. I am thinking of James Maxwell as I approach the dock. *We would be there.*

Mendacities of the Media.

We would be there tomorrow, again, after the trip was done. For the sake of the radio programmes, we would pretend to be arriving at the dock again, tomorrow, after the trip was done. But in the event we could not use the recording, since it was technologically impossible to erase the joy from our voices, that we had *been* there before and would never *be* there again.

The Gullborg *leaves harbour.* Jamesson will learn that the boat is thirty-five years old, and that one of the crew has been on it for forty years. But then, he knows much he does not understand. The most fish they ever caught in a single day was 105 tons, in 1981. Jamesson will see a photograph of them in celebration.

We leave harbour on the *Gullborg.* Cold, trepidation, great engulfing fondness for Heimaey, the only town on the Westman Isles. In 1973 a mountain assaulted it. Everybody survived, spirit of Heimaey. Now the townspeople look wise and the mountain incorrigible, sulky. We have been here twenty-four hours, it's tiny and strange, it's an endless Sunday afternoon in South Wales, but we love it, we miss it, every black volcanic fistful of it, every lonely video shop and shuttered garage and deserted street of it. It's gone. We've gone. So we sway on the deck and we need our radio equipment, we test it, we caress it, we use it. *Everything we say will be accurate because of it!*

Petersson: Shouldn't we be putting this on Absolute Time?
Jamesson: One, one, one, one . . .
Petersson: Why won't it pause?
Jamesson: One two, two one, one two, two one . . .

73

Simon's maintaining a sort of flesh colour and we're halfway to the Faroe Isles, Jamesson addresses imaginary Radio 3 listeners. And now for some music.

> *Clydesdale,* his fleet-wing'd gallant ship,
> Upon the waters seemed to skip . . .
> Then with a swift though gentle motion
> Glided on the peaceful ocean.
> Unto the west of Ireland bound,
> Swift flew the plunging paddles round;
> The gentle zephyrettic gale
> With easy vigour swelled the sail . . .

Jamesson, on the trawler *Gullborg* rather than the ferry *Clydesdale*, relives his ancestor's experience of the sea, but fails to recognise the skipping on the water, the gentleness, the peacefulness or the ease. He cannot speak for their destination, or the direction of the wind. A zephyrettic sounds like what Petersson needs right now, two of them, dissolved in water. Plink, plink, fizz.

I live as far from the sea as an Englishman possibly could live.

Gulls getting the drift, hanging off, silent. Boat engine chugs already sickeningly, oil and salt in the air. One of us always staring, homesick, at the city lights of the DAT recorder we learned to use in a warm studio at BBC Bristol, the other worriedly out at the tilting sea. Then we swap. One of us is starting to hate it. The one who isn't hating it yet feels a little sick and observes to the captain, 'It's looking a bit rough to us.' *Oh no, no. Thought it would be worse.*

Inside the cabin is Frederik the helmsman: *I speak not English!* No, you bellow it. Later he will bellow to Jamesson in confidence, in the teeth of the gale, *White Hart Lane! Notting Hamforest!* The captain, wiry and taciturn. His sons, friendly teenagers in rock-band tour T-shirts. Didn't think we were still on that planet. But hi-tech machines everywhere: computers, radar, steering equipment. Charts on the walls. The lads listen to the weather forecast and nod. Petersson, no translation necessary, leaves the cabin abruptly. He has an appointment with the worst day of his life, and can't be late, and can't be helped.

Jamesson breaks the ice.

Where are we? *West of the Westman Isles, about eight miles.* So that's halfway to America? *Ha, ha. No.*

Jamesson shows an interest in Nordic politics and the employment patterns of the Westman Isles.

Are you expecting any problems with Norwegians? *Ha, ha. No.* Er . . . do you get much time to enjoy yourself? *Oh yes, I am an electrician.*

Jamesson of the BBC.

You've obviously got to start fishing in a few minutes, so how do you feel?

The water is not very still, observes the Second Mate. In the cabin: Frederik at the helm, enjoying the bad weather, rolling with it. Off the cabin: tiny sleeping quarters, to which Jamesson retires when not recording, to compose himself by lying down. Otherwise he will be sick. He is never sick and is determined to fight it. He can count the times he has been sick on the fingers of one hand. Later he will be. Below: engine room. Below that: galley. Other six crew members playing cards and eating breakfast when not out on deck catching fish. Breakfast is skyr, revolting Icelandic yoghurt. Revolting even on land, in that world. But kindly offered to Jamesson. Must be joking. Off the galley: sickbay. Darkness, strange unpleasant smell of fruit. One of the crew has entered Jamesson's quarters and said: *Your friend would like to see you* . . .

Jamesson sees his friend, a pale face at the far end of a dark closet.

You recording, Max? *Yep.* We've been at sea about – what, two hours now? *Yeah, bit more, bit more* . . .

Jamesson hears his friend.

This is just, completely, unspeakably unpleasant, and I just want to wake up and for everything to go away . . . we're supposed to come on this trip for some experience – all I've seen is a guy go past the cabin door eating a carrot – that can't be right, can it?

> Soon all on board retired to sleep
> Save those that must the night-watch keep . . .
> Those on deck must stay perforce
> To guide and guard their nightly course.

You've obviously got to start fishing.

Seven times they go out, the six men, while Helmsman Frederik watches them, grinning, from the cabin. Every time the boat leans more than 45° from the vertical his grin widens like a kind of geophysiognomical reaction, and then he roars happily to Jamesson in Icelandic. Jamesson, sick and scared, gathering ghostly Radio 3 listeners around him so as to depict the practices of Icelandic cod fishing for their benefit, essays the wannest smile since Oates said to Scott at the South Pole: 'Never mind, Robert, now we can concentrate on the League.'

Okay, I'm going out where the action is.

Working BBC Freelancer: Hey, you have a message for the people of England there? *Working Cod Fisherman:* Here's your fish and chips! *Freelancer:* Ha ha ha! Ha, ha! Ha. Hmm . . .

Okay, I'm out there now.

First Man – hooks the fish out of the sea into a long net, then on to a conveyor belt which moves across the deck. Second Man – slits the fish and throws the innards out to the sea, hence the gulls. Third Man – clubs the fish (somewhat superfluously, it occurs to our correspondent) and throws them in a box. Fourth and Fifth Men – feed the net back into the sea. Sixth Man – miscellaneous tasks: hosing the blood off the deck, hosing the blood off the others, laughing at the Seventh Man: *Here you see Icelandic slaves!*

Dress: Orange plastic armour.

Seventh Man (optional) – Recording the noise of three tons of Atlantic cod being slit, clubbed and generally slapped around, for the benefit of the BBC's classical music station. But, as correspondent reflects in rare moment of perspicacity, it's difficult to know what to say about it for seven more hours.

Dress: M&S anoraks, headphones, a DAT recorder and microphone with sodden fur hood, like Dougal from 'The Magic Roundabout' having been forcibly held underwater.

On-deck activities of Jamesson, tied to mast of Gullborg:

– Remembering time when he sat alone in his bedroom in Welwyn, writing sonnets.

– Considering career as quantity surveyor.

– Reciting from *The Orators:* 'O Bulldog Drummond, protect us, O Green Man, protect us . . .' Reflecting that he'd like to have seen Auden try this.

– Recalling Petersson, from what seems many weeks ago.

– Singing 'For Those in Peril on the Sea'.

– Being honest: 'You've never had a mad British man sitting on deck before, have you?'

What Jamesson's ancestor did:

> But O! how brief is earthly bliss!
> What scene must now succeed to this! . . .
> 'Fire! fire!' Loud – louder rings the cry!
> Affrighted sleep fled – every eye
> Is open! At the Captain's word
> Are quickly seen 'All hands aboard.'
> At every pump the seamen strain –
> The flame withstands their efforts vain . . .

'[Maxwell] struck one hand upon his heart, as he flung the other above his head, and with uplifted eyes uttered, "Oh, God Almighty, enable me to do my duty!" . . . and instantly taking the helm, fixed himself on the spot.'

Chambers' Edinburgh Journal, May 9, 1835

I've got to have a break . . . euh my God . . . it's really – here we go – euh my God . . .

> Yet, see the gallant Maxwell stand,
> With burning rudder in his hand,
> The still-determined hero guides
> And hurls the vessel through the tides!

'At intervals the motion of the wind threw aside the intervening mass of flame and smoke for a moment, and then might be heard exclamations of hope and gratitude as the multitude on the prow got a glimpse of the brave man standing calm and fixed on his dreadful watch!'

Chambers' Edinburgh Journal, May 9, 1835

Jamesson called upon to be a Hero too.

Fisherman: Do you think you can have lunch with us?

> And thrice shrill groans of deep despair
> With mingled terror rent the air . . .

Er . . . I'll try. *Okay, you try. Hey, he'll try!*

After seven catches, the fishing is done. In the real world it is about noon. Jamesson has his commentary and his 'wildtrack', and his stomach holding out and holding in, as lunch lurches into nostril range. Petersson has been offered a Garibaldi biscuit – 'and that was me out for another two hours.'

Lunch with us.

The men sit down to feast on stew and chips. Jamesson, whose insides are not only fomenting revolt, but have installed an interim government and renamed the year *Zero*, takes snapshots of the crew eating – anything to avoid joining them. Frederik is there too, leading Jamesson suddenly to wonder who's piloting the thing. Visions of his Ancestor swim before him, and headlines in the Nordic press: POET STEERS MAD FISHERMEN HOME.

> The flames that issue from the wreck
> Are roasting Maxwell on the deck;
> But, O! not this his heart dismays,
> He calmly stands amid the blaze
> With hope depicted in his eyes,
> As on the burning vessel flies . . .

As it happens, my great-great-great-grandfather saved the lives of everybody on board the *Clydesdale*, off Corswall Point, Galloway, on an autumn night in 1827, by steering the burning ship through a twelve-yard gap in the rocks and on to the beach, as his hair turned grey and his skin was roasted and he was maimed for life.

'Though the flames had not actually closed around [Maxwell] as he stood on his awful watch, yet such was the heat under him and around him, that not only, as I have said, were his feet severely burnt, but his hair, a large hair-cap, and huge dreadnought watch-coat, which he wore, were all in such a state from the intense heat, that they crumbled into powder on the least touch.'

Chambers' Edinburgh Journal, May 9, 1835

James Maxwell was my first hero, and 'The Pilot Maxwell', such as it is, was the first poem I remember. I did think of him a lot in the storm, just to keep mind and body together, but of course I took one look at Frederik wolfing his chips, having first dipped them in stew, and, well, it was a first for Radio 3 listeners . . .

The Return of Petersson.

This is Not Very Able Seaman Armitage . . . just ventured up on deck for the second time after the worst day of his life . . . nine hours of extreme nausea . . . every now and again I could hear the blokes in the kitchen – I heard the word 'Englander' then a lot of laughing . . . I think that about sums it up. I can see land now, through one of the windows – it's just – joyous.

Petersson Crazed With Relief, Part I.

Actually, I'm feeling all right now! Maybe we should turn around.

Jamesson's Bleak Look, Part I.

Maybe not.

Petersson Crazed With Relief, Part II.

I've absolutely no idea what's been going on while I've been on this boat – we could have caught nothing, we could have caught a killer whale, I've no idea. Slashing down with rain . . . like being in somebody's stomach . . . I'm feeling quite maritime now. Have they caught some fish?

Jamesson's Bleak Look, Part II.

'Have they caught some fish?' 'Have they caught some fish?'

We love the Westman Isles.

The Westman Isles are still, they don't move, they have colours other than grey and orange, they have sounds other than engine, they have smells other than oil and vomit, they have warmth, they have women, they have MTV. We love the Westman Isles because they're Iceland, which is land, which is England, which is home, which doesn't move and is still, and is one day going to be the present.

Public Declarations.

Jamesson: Thanks, that was a real pleasure – it's been memorable.
Petersson: Thanks, it's been terrific..

Private Declarations.

Petersson: Back on dry land – walking around here – bit shaky – it's really good!
Jamesson: Simon, can I just recap . . . It's over.

A Sailor Stoppeth Jamesson

You will be there.
What things are there
Will suck through you.
This you must do.

You will get up.
What waves come up
Have come for you.
Make them make do.

You will go out.
What light goes out
Goes out on you.
It's happy to.

You'll be afraid.
What's not afraid
Knows what to do.
But not for you.

You will fall sick.
What made you sick
Was some of you.
Cough that adieu.

You will despair.
When you despair
I'll think of you.
I'll know you do.

But you'll come home.
Why that must be
Not the vast sea
Vouchsafed to me.

Song of the West Men

To the far of the far
off the isles of the isles,
near the rocks of the rocks
which the guillemots stripe
with the shite of their shite,

a trawler went down
in the weave of the waves,
and a fisherman swam
for the life of his life
through the swell of the sea

which was one degree C.
And the bones of his bones
were cooler than stone,
and the tide of his blood
was slower than slow.

He met with the land
where the cliffs of the cliffs
were steeper than sheer,
where the sheep had to graze
by the teeth of their teeth.

So he put out again
for the beach,
and made it to lava
that took back his skin
to the feet of his feet,

and arrived at a door
with a tenth of a tale
that was taller than tall,
as cold and as bled as a man
from a fridge. But he lived.

The good of the good
will come this way, they say:
tattered and torn,
unlikely and out of the storm
if it comes at all.

St Giles' Day

Birthday of John Bunyan – Pilgrim's Progress

For breakfast they managed a slice of dry toast and a beaker of water between them, then shuffled down to the quayside. Mr Rosmundsson had promised that the trip would be cancelled if the weather was bad, but unfortunately the clouds were lifting and the sun was beginning to break through. The crew of the *Gullborg* were taking provisions on board as the captain came down the gangplank to meet them, admiring their recording equipment and informing them that his boat was the most successful trawler on the island, having once netted over a hundred tons of cod in a single day. Its name, in Icelandic, meant El Dorado. Apart from the pilot who was in his sixties, the rest of the crew were young men, two of them brothers, and they all grinned the same toothy grin when Petersson and Jamesson explained that this was their first time on a fishing boat. All anoraks were buttoned and zipped, all wind-shields were tightly laced around the microphones, and names and addresses of loved ones were left on dry land before the boat chugged out of the bottle-neck harbour making for the grey horizon.

Sailing for the open sea, Jamesson began recalling a certain amount of seafaring history on his father's side of the family, whereas Petersson was descended from a long line of landlubbers of the first water, and as a precaution had already swallowed double the recommended dose of Sea-Legs as well as attaching a 'Travel Band' to each of his wrists, a device designed to apply acupressure to the Nei-Kuan point, thereby reducing the effects of nausea or morning sickness.

The boat couldn't have been more than half a mile from land when it swung round forty-five degrees into the oncoming waves, a move which seemed to coincide with a change in the weather.

One second the prow was pointing into the stormy heavens, the next it was heading for the seabed, with a wall of water quivering above it, and it was during one such movement that Petersson's body and soul parted company. They were reunited momentarily, only for his stomach and its contents to go their separate ways as the boat attempted a vertical take-off, and ten seconds later he was dragged by one of the crew to the 'sickbay', a horizontal broom cupboard somewhere below the water-line, to be seen once more in the next nine hours, when he ventured back up into the daylight and was immediately reacquainted with last night's pepperoni pizza.

Up on deck, Able Seaman Jamesson lashed himself to the mast, and for the rest of the day recorded the sounds of cod being hauled from the water, coshed on the head, gutted in front of his eyes and tossed into the ice-house. It was only when the cook produced a bowl of soup of unspecified origins that he succumbed to the inevitable. Just before sunset, as the boat was rounding the headland for Heimaey harbour, Petersson surfaced from his darkened room and asked a gut-smeared and blood-stained Mr Jamesson if any fish had been caught. His reply was captured on tape, but deemed unsuitable at the end of the day for transmission on national network radio.

Back on shore, Petersson was told by the youngest member of the crew that when he first started on the trawler his own seasickness had lasted for five months, but there was no other work for him on the island. Finally conquering it, he took a week's holiday somewhere on the mainland, but was sick again for another month after returning to work. If it had been within his powers, Petersson would have awarded him the Victoria Cross and the Congressional Medal of Honor there and then, for fortitude beyond the scope of human imagination. Another crew member had just enough English to ask if there were any tickets left for the Pink Floyd concert at Wembley in November.

¶

From where we stand
the sea as it was
is a soup

of beasts: fish
with feathers and wings,
sabre-toothed, three-legged things.

Head-on, a capelin
with its face gone wrong,
and the fox turned white

at the coming of man.
Bears from the pole
fetch up

on presentation plinths
of snow,
and a godsend here

is a stranded whale,
a gift
of blubber and oil.

1 Horse

2 'Two Fools at Gullfoss'

3 Left to right: Sjón, Bragi Ólafsson, Jamesson, Petersson ('a huge flash of white light for a face'), Steinunn Sigurdardóttir, Einar Kárason

4 After the reading at the Café Sólon Íslandus. Left to right: Sjón, Jamesson, Petersson, Sigfus Bjartmarsson

5 'The water is not very still'

6 Jamesson and Squeaky at Fljótstunga above the Toblerone cabins

7 Duet, Kalmunstunga

8 Snowcats

9 Roadhouse, Myvatn

10 Near Krafla

11 Petersson interviewing the North Atlantic

12 Evensong, Breiðavik Church

13 Furthest point west, the danger signs

14 Homesickness, Breiðavik Bay

Sweet Home Reykjavík

You drove cos you didn't mind and I didn't mind
you drove a million miles
and we listened to what I said cos you didn't mind
and that was to Dylan always
then we listened to what you said cos I didn't mind
and that was the Lemonheads album
then I counted the number of fjords to be still gone round
and that was still twenty-nine

and we did a whole one in silence except for the sound
of us thinking ahead to the next one
and we did a whole coastline laughing we didn't mind
though I can't remember what at though
so I counted the number of fjords to be still gone round
and that was still twenty-six still
so we listened to what we agreed I could scrabble and find
Violently Happy, Venus as a Boy –

thus we brought our two lives back in the back of the car
tapping us asking *How long now?*
and I counted the number of fjords to be still sick for
and it was still twenty-six
and we did a whole one in silence except for the whirr
of our poems in helicopters
and old sex flinging itself on the windscreen there
look at me look at me uncle

and Reykjavík Reykjavík after our being so far
that toddling town, Big Herring,
we couldn't wait, it was *Expo, the World's Fair*
we couldn't wait, we were abseiling

fjord to fjord the fair length of Iceland's hair
to get to a beer, girls pouring,
jealousy, litter, the realm of the sip and stare,
scant love but light enough.

Friday

At the food-tasting session back at Reykjavík's Bummannssklukkan Restaurant, head chef Matthías swept into the upstairs lounge with an assortment of national dishes and local delicacies, none of them instantly recognisable. Having drawn the short straw, Mr Jamesson removed the cocktail stick from a cube of calf's head, and passed it carefully from one side of his mouth to the other. Once he had satisfied himself that it was free from eyelashes and teeth, he reported a not-unpleasant taste and helped himself to another lump. Mr Petersson opted for what looked like a slice of ham, and had just popped it into his mouth when Matthías finally translated it as womb of lamb. Although Petersson couldn't consider himself a vegetarian, he realised at this point that his appetite for animals was generally limited to the outer two or three inches of a beast, and even if he had eaten some of the more abstract inner organs during the course of his life he drew the line at a creature's gynaecological equipment. He swallowed it without chewing, but the thought of it stayed with him for much of the afternoon.

Next came the braised puffin, which both men sampled and were broadly in favour of. It was a comfort for Petersson to think that the birds he had hurled to their death only days before might not have died in vain, but Jamesson had to wonder about the attitude of a nation that ate one of its national symbols. Imagine tucking into topside of bulldog back at home, or wandering into an American diner and ordering a bald-eagle burger. Last up was the dried catfish, cut into strips, hung out on frames and left to cure in the freezing wind. Its texture was somewhere between old insole and medium-density fibreboard, but once broken down its flavour was that of any other fish left out on a washing line for two years before being passed through an industrial mangle. They thanked Matthías for an extra-ordinary culinary experience, pocketed a fistful of toothpicks and set out through the streets of the city in search of fruit and vegetables.

After sleeping off lunch, Petersson scraped three days of stubble from his face, worked a gobbet of gel into his hair, and tried to take the creases from his best shirt with the toy iron provided by the hotel. He met with Jamesson in the lobby, where they chose ties from a selection thoughtfully provided by Mr Jamesson senior, and helped each other with the knots like one man dressing himself in front of a mirror. In the car they compared notes and went over their list of questions, reminding themselves that they had been advised to steer clear of overtly political subjects, but adamant at the same time that they didn't want just to talk about the weather. They parked up and wandered along what they thought was the right street, but eventually had to ask for directions, and followed the pointed finger of a six-year-old boy on a bike to a white, one-storey wooden building surrounded by a small strip of lawn. There they were shown to a waiting-room and offered coffee, and sat for five minutes, double-checking their equipment and biting their fingernails, until a tall man in a camel suit came in through a door behind them, and said 'The President will see you now.'

Extracts from an Interview

... with Vigdís Finnbogadóttir, President of Iceland

SA: Am I right in saying that you are the first democratically elected female head of state in the world?

VF: As a matter of fact it is true, and I am very proud of my Icelanders to have had the guts and the courage to take this step, and be the pioneers. It was sixteen years ago – it was world news. I received a clipping from a Chinese newspaper with my picture in the middle, not knowing what this woman was doing on the front page. And now if a woman is elected somewhere it doesn't make world news, so the world has changed in that respect in little over a decade. I was the Artistic Director of the City Theatre of Reykjavík for eight years before coming into office. People from foreign countries are often very surprised when they hear that I came from the theatre, and they ask how on earth a person can jump from the arts to become the president of a country, and my answer to that is that you cannot study how to become a president, there is no university where you can enlist and learn how to become such a person. But in the theatre, in the literary and performing side of the arts, you can study life from all sides, and what is a presidency about if not people and life?

SA: You've already answered the question I was going to ask – about the career move. But how did it come about? What was the process?

VF: It has in a way become a tradition within our fifty years of freedom and of the Independent Republic of Iceland, that the people look for their presidents among the intellectuals within the humanistic field. My predecessor was an archaeologist – he was the curator of the National Museum. It's very important for the

93

people to see in their president someone who can talk about their identity, and identity is not composed of political parties. Identity comes from heritage and from the living memory of the people – of the generations. We have very deep roots in this country, because we remember how it all began here, how it all started eleven hundred years ago, and we have a language between us which is the only classical language still spoken in Europe. All the other languages alive today have changed from their Latin and Greek and Germanic roots, but we are still speaking the language that was spoken in the Nordic countries in the ninth century and before. We are like flowers or plants or trees with very deep roots in the soil of this island country. The language and the memory – they are the two factors that compose our identity.

GM: From everyone we've spoken to – in many different fields – we get the impression that a thousand years of European history have happened in a hundred years here in Iceland. Are you afraid that if things continue at such a pace, you'll be bombarded by outside influences and the things which are uniquely Icelandic will be eroded? Do you feel you have to fight for them in some way?

VF: Yes, in the same way that people anywhere have to fight for their values. Everywhere in the world, not least in Europe, we have to pause and think of values. Speaking quite frankly, I think there are relatively few people in officialdom who think about values and talk about values. There is a trend in the world to think first and foremost about economy, about the strength of the economy, and of course we have to have a strong economy. But in the shadow of that wish for growth we must never forget to mention and to be reminded of other values as well. I would really like to establish an international association of those who want to speak about values – can you help me do that one day? It has never been as important as it is in this open society of ours – which is so open because of the mass media – to discuss values, and to point out values other than money.

GM: Another value that I know is important to you is the value of preserving the natural beauty of Iceland. In the *Book Of Settlements* it says that the first settlers found a land where the trees stretched from the mountains to the sea, but now there is a joke which says 'What do you do if you find yourself lost in an Icelandic forest? Stand up!' We've driven for miles and not seen any trees – to what extent are you part of the attempts to redress this?

VF: I'm very much part of that, because wherever I go I go with my trees and I plant them. I also make the country greener by sowing grass. We live in a very eroded country, and when the settlers came here eleven hundred years ago it was so much greener, and through that time we have lost two thirds of the green of Iceland, which is a lot. There are three factors leading to this: wind, volcanic eruptions (some of the land is now under lava) and the third is human habitation, because some of the vegetation is very vulnerable in this country. Now we have the ambition to turn the volcanic desert into a green land, the ambition to turn black sand into green grass. And if we can do it we can set an example.

GM: We've been to the house where Reagan and Gorbachev had their summit meeting, and also in recent years the Norwegians helped to build bridges between countries in the Middle East, and I was wondering whether you thought that countries like Iceland with an extraordinary history of peace can help larger nations come together and resolve their problems without brutality and violence and destruction and so on.

VF: Well, certainly the Icelanders are a very peaceful people. But at this point I think we can be of greatest use by doing things well – for instance, with the fishing industry – in convincing ourselves and others that the Earth can be taken care of, and be made green and fruitful. I can imagine an international centre in Iceland to distribute this knowledge, this know-how. Being realistic, I see this more as Iceland's role, since we are so few, and since everything is measured in size. And I am of the belief that Iceland has to be visited to be understood. It is impossible to imagine that a nation of two hundred and fifty thousand can do the things that we are doing here, and I know from experience that when somebody wants to come here and construct something, the Icelanders are asked 'How many engineers shall we bring?', and we say 'We have them.' 'How many technicians shall we bring?' 'We have them.' And 'How many workers?' 'We have them.' Every single individual has a use in a small society such as ours, but since the world doesn't understand this I'm afraid they wouldn't look to us as somebody to negotiate in peace matters.

SA: Iceland, geographically and geologically, exists at a very special place in the world where two continents, as it were, are pulling apart, and it also seems to occupy a very elevated position, looking down on the rest of the world. Do you think this is reflected in the consciousness of the people? Do you think their perceptions and perspectives are affected by those things?

VF: Well, it is very charming to hear you say this, because we *are* sitting on the top of the world, of course, with a very extraordinary view, on the peak up here. I like to compare it with Odin. You'll remember that he was sitting at the top of the world and had two ravens which he sent out every day – one was mind and one was memory – and they came back at night and sat on his shoulders and whispered news into his ears. This is the situation of Iceland – sat on top of the world and looking and following closely everything that's happening.

¶

From where we stand
the birch is at one
with itself

in the wood,
seeds are sown
by aircraft

from above.
Surtsey dreams
of a beard

of grass,
the northern orchid
practises its curtsey

near the primrose path.
Fireweed holds its own,
but ash and willow

pick their way
on tip-toe
through a spoil of stone.

Fljótstunga

We're bushed and happy who crossed in our new invention
An ashen plain: he drove and I navigated,
We chatted away in the sunlessness, we found
To our great gladness this the first one of the farms,
Our pillow-hall! and making our way all smiles
Towards the dark meat smell of a special cooking –
We met both our mothers here in that, and the welcome
Reserved for sons who arrive just this side of nightfall.

St Gregory the Great's Day

They could have been looking at a small distillery at the head of a Scottish loch when they finally clapped eyes on Iceland's last remaining whaling station, 'mothballed' for the time being but ready to swing into action at a moment's notice, apparently. They wandered around the site giving a spontaneous commentary into the microphone, without really knowing what they were looking for or what it would look like if they found it. The main feature of the station was an enormous slipway running down into the water, stained with what they described as blood but was probably rust from the heavy-duty chain that ran the length of the ramp. Elsewhere, a generator buzzed in one of the huts, and a sign depicting an inquisitive civilian with a thunderbolt through his upper body warned against taking a look inside. There was no one around to speak to, no skeleton staff keeping the knives sharp and the fires burning, and no restless spirits to play havoc with the equipment or register on the VU meter. They left the place exactly as they had found it, with the water calm and unruffled along the shoreline.

Another two hours' driving inland, often on roads that were river-beds punctuated with pot-holes and pontoon bridges, brought them eventually to Fljótstunga, for their first taste of farmhouse hospitality. Sat on the front step for supper, they looked out on a landscape that could have been the backcloth for an epic film: an opal ice-cap in the far distance, with six or seven perfectly conical volcanoes nestled underneath it. In front of those, a lava field of broken rock split diagonally by a slow, grey river, and down beneath them a mile or so of meadows and fields rising all the way to their feet. The farm dog, who sounded as if he might have been called 'Squeaky', waited patiently for biscuit crumbs and pats on the head. Pets, they decided, were the essential difference between staying in hotels and staying in houses, and Petersson slipped Squeaky an extra Rich Tea in recognition of that fact.

Supper was a fairly challenging combination of boiled lamb and curry sauce, and they were joined at the table by four Swiss-German fishermen wielding a litre of wine that went no further than their own glasses. As the meal progressed, it transpired their fellow guests didn't just fish the river behind the farm, they owned it, and the one with the alcoholic complexion and ginger moustache began a long and unrewarding tale of which he was the hero, transporting salmon or trout beyond the waterfall in the back of his Range Rover. At the end of his story, all four of them lifted their glasses for a toast, and the stone-cold sober poets chinked their tumblers of rain water together, muttering 'Cheers' through clenched teeth. Later that night, however, there was great joy in the Petersson/Jamesson camp when a bottle of duty-free citrus vodka was discovered inside a microphone sock, and the evening was saved. Once the Swiss-Germans had disappeared down the slope to their Toblerone-shaped cabins, the bottle was opened and Squeaky joined them on the veranda for a nightcap. 'Prost,' said Mr Jamesson under his breath, as the sun melted into the ice-cap on the horizon and a million stars that had waited their turn all afternoon came steadily into contention.

After breakfast, they were driven by the farmer in his shooting-brake along a dirt track through the lava field, then helped unload a number of ropes and spikes and clips, and set off walking to the right across the broken rocks with Squeaky bringing up the rear. They arrived at a large crater where the crust of the Earth had collapsed, and scrambled down into it, making towards a tunnel at the far end that opened into a small cave with water dripping atmospherically from the roof and a sheet of thick ice underfoot. The farmer slid on his stomach to the darkest and narrowest end of the cave, and began hammering iron pegs into the ice and threading a rope between them, and with the help of the flashlight it was possible to see a black hole beyond him, like a throat, with stalactites dangling down like tonsils. It was also becoming obvious that one or other of them would be expected to descend with the farmer into the belly of the Earth, and bearing in mind his poor showing on the trawler, Petersson lashed the rope to his belt, turned on the lamp on his caving helmet, and slithered to the edge of the ice, looking down into the gullet of blackness.

The farmer had rigged up a rope ladder, and following him down it Petersson arrived in another tunnel, and could see the farmer on his hands and knees about twenty or thirty yards ahead. After he had caught up with him, they scurried along the passageway for some distance, then stood up in an enormous cavern where the walls and the roof were beyond the reach of their torches and the only things that showed in the beams of light were water droplets, falling like diamonds through the air. They stumbled to what looked like the back of the cavern, and up a pile of rocks that had obviously fallen from the roof, but on shining his light into the distance beyond him Petersson could see further and further passageways, and he stayed close to the farmer, not wanting to end up as three column inches under an alliterative newspaper headline back at home. Before escaping from the underworld, Petersson lifted a small piece of lava rock from the floor, as a souvenir or *memento mori*, and was about to pocket it when the farmer gave him a look which would have meant 'no' in any language. With what little English he had, he explained that to take anything from the cave would be to offend the trolls, and with what little Icelandic *he* had Petersson said that he was very sorry, even though rock was a commodity that didn't seem in short supply in these parts, and put the precious object back in its rightful position. Breaking surface over the top rung of the rope ladder, he reached for what he took to be Jamesson's outstretched helping hand, only to discover the head of a microphone and half a dozen clever comments on the themes of Dante, Orpheus, Perseus, Jules Verne, Arthur Scargill and Stig of the Dump, in that order.

Before leaving they signed the visitors' book that William Morris had signed over a century before them, and were amazed when Mrs Fljótstunga Farm produced a hardback anthology of Icelandic women's poetry, *And Then It Rained Flowers*, of which she was the contributing editor. As she went out to feed the sheep, the two of them were humbled enough to sign and leave copies of their own slim paperback volumes on the hall table, looking like pamphlets alongside her own slab of work, illustrated with star-daisies and forget-me-nots and bound in a square foot or more of animal skin.

Next stop was Kalmunstunga, half a mile away, where Auden and MacNeice had played the very piano on which the Icelandic national anthem was composed, and they knocked at the door with their recording equipment held out in front of them. The lady of the house couldn't have known if they were market researchers or government officials come to check radiation levels under the floorboards, but she showed them inside in any event, and shooed her three children into the next room, leaving the piano at their disposal. The thing itself was upright, German in origin, and after tinkering around on it for a couple of minutes and setting up the microphones, they sat down on the stools provided and set about the one song that they both knew: 'Perfect Day', by Lou Reed, from the *Transformer* album. After a promising start they lost the thread on a minor chord somewhere in the middle eight, and the rendition ended in a fit of giggles and a handful of bum notes. As they thanked the householder and left the premises, she waved goodbye as if what had gone on there couldn't have been more ordinary, and her three children filed back into the living-room to watch television.

The last event of the day was a visit to the glacier, where they were obliged to dress in day-glo orange Soviet spacesuits and fifties sci-fi crash helmets before taking charge of their two-man 'snowcat' and jetting off across the ice, the vehicle itself being a hybrid combination of motorbike, sidecar and amphibious landing-craft. They followed the guide up to the summit, peered over the edge into a bottomless fissure, then after agreeing with him that they wouldn't like to fall down it skidooed back to the cabin and dismounted. Then having driven for an hour in the car they stopped and looked back at the glacier, and thought they could still see him, the snowcat operator, twenty-five miles away in his tangerine all-in-one, on his own under a mountain of ice, waiting for the next customer.

Song of the Interiorites

From the fissures and faults
and the eyries and peaks,
from the clints and grikes
and corries and creeks
there's a river runs east,
and a vessel that leaves
every three or four weeks
but there's death half a dozen times over
downstream, downstream, and then there's the sea.

There's a stretch without breeze
through a plain without trees
where a ketch under sail
can be lulled into sleep,
and banks of sand
where a craft might beach,
where many a sloop
comes to rest in peace.
There's death half a dozen times over
downstream, downstream, and then there's the sea.

That cloud of dust
is a googol of gnats,
mosquitoes and fleas
that can pick a bone clean
in a minute flat,
reduce a man to tears, if that,
a month of supplies
to the stone of a peach.
There's death half a dozen times over
downstream, downstream, and then there's the sea.

And hornets as well. And bees.
And rapids, ravines,
and falls like the falls
at the edge of the world,
and rocks underneath
with sabre-tooth teeth
that can scalpel a yawl
down the seam of its keel.
There's death half a dozen times over
downstream, downstream, and then there's the sea.

There's life in the drink
from a darker age,
from the dinosaur days:
unspeakable fish, unfeasible beasts,
oysters and clams
with tonsils and tongues,
hideous, pink, unpronounceable things
from the depths of the deep.
There's death half a dozen times over
downstream, downstream, and then there's the sea.

There's a geyser that blows
that can balance a skiff
like a seal with a ball
on the knob of its nose,
and lava that flows
from the core of the globe
that can catch a boat napping
and set it in stone.
There's death half a dozen times over
downstream, downstream, and then there's the sea.

There's a confluence point
just a mile from the coast;
pack-ice and slush
from the Arctic north
meet the sulphur and mush
from the thermal pools;
one river thaws
where another one cools,
boats disappear
in a simmering goop
of luminous bubbles,
poisonous steam.
There's death half a dozen times over
downstream, downstream, and then there's the sea.

Death half a dozen times over at least
downstream, and then there's the sea.

The White Hart

It comes to me first against the green of the trees, a kind of vacancy, not the creature itself but a whiteness in the image of the creature. As if it had sensed me and moved on, leaving a pure emptiness in its place.

Last night in the cabin, I took a pair of scissors to the one and only photograph of the white hart, a picture I'd taken years ago, by accident. I'd been tracking in the high forest, following footprints for the sake of it. I was sitting down on a stone, pouring tea from a flask and eating the bread in my pocket. It was early evening. The view was a good one – a long sweep of cleared ground rising to a narrow valley, becoming a deep ravine carved out by water, with a summit beyond. So I walked back to a pile of rocks and mounted my camera, lining it up for a self-portrait. I'd just flicked the switch when I looked up, and it was standing there in front of me, right in frame, powerful over every moment that followed, as if it had brought the planet to a halt under its feet. The timer uncoiled through its countdown of ten seconds, the flash-bulb christened everything with silver and the shutter clicked. The white hart turned away into the trees and the earth began spinning on its axis again.

Last night in the cabin I sank the point of the scissors into the photograph, making an incision just under its throat. Then I cut along its outline, letting the two steel blades eat away at the print; down the line of its breast, up and down the legs, along its spine, between the trunk and branches of the antlers and around the curve of its muzzle, holding the scissors firm and straight in my right hand, steering the picture with my left. I pinned the cut-out to the door, pushing a bradawl through the animal's head into the soft wood behind. And I held the hollowed-out photograph up to the window, filling the shape of the white hart with the dark shades of the moving sky.

I have brought this about, made it happen. The white hart stands in the foreground, no more than fifty yards away. When it steps sideways and swings its head it becomes real, and bones and muscles move under its skin. I remember the photograph, its eyes looking right through the lens to a focal point somewhere in the back of my head. I lift the rifle into my shoulder, but in the time it takes to bring the barrel to eye-level the target has disappeared into the distance, away into the cleared ground towards the ravine and the summit, picking its way through tree stumps and dead wood, out of range. I sling the rifle over my back and set out, tracking the hoof-prints up and over the first ridge.

There seems to be a fixed distance between us, too far to bring it down with a clean shot, close enough never to give up the hunt. If I move quickly for a minute or more, the animal is no nearer. If the going is slow, uphill or difficult underfoot, or if I stop to catch my breath and let my blood settle, when I look up the white hart is no further in front, waiting for me a hundred yards ahead, turning away again into the background. Sometimes the animal is leading, hauling me up the gulleys and dragging me across the face of the earth. The next minute I have it reined in, holding it back with the anchor of my own weight. As it enters the ravine, kicking its way through the loose rocks in the dry stream, it is the most obvious thing in the world, more apparent than a full moon in a winter sky, the one object of light in a landscape barely alive.

I have no clear impression of the white hart. Even the photograph was blurred, soft-focus, the animal caught in the first moment of melting away into the trees. I have no mental picture of its features, no opinion of its height or weight, no image of its face other than its two dark eyes. I try to think of it dead at my feet, try to see the bullet hole punched like a precious stone in its head, but nothing comes to mind. All I know is its colour, the colour white, which is no colour at all or the colour of all light together. We come out above the stream, hunter and hunted, under the peak of the mountain, above the tree-line now and away from loose shale and scree, still climbing but more gently, heading into the land, stepping up through the contours, into altitude, letting the lower world sink down behind us out of sight. The white hart waits on the verge of the sky, as black as the universe, in silhouette against the light of day.

My breath comes alive in front of my face, then evaporates. I take a hip flask from an inside pocket, fill the tiny cap with strong, clear spirit and pour the liquid into my throat, with my head back and my eyes in the sun. The alcohol unravels in my chest, like cold air drawn into the lungs, and my next breath is a haze of fumes and smoke and steam. I say the words 'white hart', and watch them rise into the heavens, weightless. Between here and the skyline the animal waits, watches me thread the lid of the flask and tuck it back in my coat. Then it turns away again and makes for the next place, towards the cover of clouds and the upper slopes.

Where the mist begins the land gives in to the cold; grass and heather galvanised in frost, surface water fixed with ice. Then snow, in hollows and drifts at first, then everywhere, up to the knees, then firmer underfoot, packed hard in layers and seams, frozen to a great depth, part of the rock. With the white hart just above me in folds of thick cloud, I can see no further than the next step, then the next. But I hear it close by, its feet striking into the ground like a chisel into stone, shocks of sound hitting down to the bedrock and back. It can only be five yards ahead at most, no more than that. I stand still, soundless, draped in the white air, drenched by it, sensing the creature only an instant away, holding my breath like a man in a tent, awake to a living thing just inches from his face, wanting to listen, not wanting to be heard. I could reach out, here, to the left, lift my arm and open my hand towards it. But I blink and it bolts, clatters away over the iron ground dragging a trail of vapour, goes high overhead then slows, till the sound of its hooves is the sound of an animal walking on a metal roof. I think about firing blind into the noise where it might be, then think again, and go on following, up inside the cloud, like parting one set of curtains after another, through to the other side.

I climb out into a wide, unlimited brightness. Behind me, an ocean of cloud comes to an end at my heels. In front, the ground and the air are the same, with no horizon slicing the last of the snow from the first of the sky. At one with the elements, white on white, invisible, the animal idles somewhere in front, the occasional thump of its feet coming up through the soles of my boots. Nothing moves, until the sun comes to the boil, brings blood to its face, and like a foal or a calf standing up on all fours for the first time, the shadow of the white hart unrolls across the surface of ice, stretches into life. It waits, a negative or cut-out held to the light. Then bends at the neck as if it were bending to drink, and meets with the tip of its nose as it would in the glass of a lake. Then jolts back, stands straight. With a finger I trace the maker's name carved in the butt of the gun, but moving with high, exaggerated steps the shadow picks up its feet and pedals away out of reach. I drink from the flask, watching the shadow's shape – a sledge of darkness hauled towards the sun when it tracks west, or side-on a black glove walking on its fingertips.

In a valley where two walls of snow close to a dead-end, the white hart shows itself again, life-size, actual, outlined in front of a slab of blue rock under a glaze of ice. Cornered, it turns and looks me flat in the face, narrows itself to the stripe of its head, its neck and its breast, its two front legs. Only the antlers show to their full height and width, years of thought grown out from the bulb of its brain. I let the cross-hairs settle on the inch of nothing between its eyes, and squeeze.

The trace of the bullet – a cable broken at full stretch. The animal lifts from the ground with the shock, then buckles and drops, collapses into the grave of its shadow lying in wait, a missing piece put finally in place.

For some hours I have been striding forward at full pace. The ice that was harder than marble underfoot turns now to something rougher, thick tufts of snow, fibrous almost, like frozen wool. When I look up, the mound of its body lies somewhere ahead, just as it did an hour ago. However many yards I make towards its blurred shape, it keeps the same distance, or becomes nearer and at the same time more remote. After a long swig from the flask I burst into a mad sprint, trying to take the distance by surprise, and manage a short gallop through mid-air, charging the target with the gun held out in front. But a snowdrift hits me like a wave, and I wade from it, numb from the waist down, working my legs with my arms, both legs cast in a heavy sleeve of snow, clamping the flesh to the bone. I wait for the blood in my toes, stand up to find that the crashed body of the white hart has gone.

To walk now is to drag the distance I've covered like a chain, miles long, each step adding another link, more weight. Facing the sheer whiteness of everywhere, I make for the only mark in sight. What appears at first like a bush or a shrub, close by, becomes a tree, hundreds of yards away, enormous by the time I reach it, the frozen wood of its ancient trunk forced up through the crust of the earth. The branches are bare of leaves, completely, and smooth, but covered in fine silver hair or fur, and the bark comes away in my hands when I start to climb.

At a height where the air becomes drowsy and thin, I harness myself with the strap of the gun, wedge both feet in a narrow fork and hook one arm up and over a higher branch. I drink, but lose hold of the flask, and hear it out as it rattles through the tree, like something of worth falling down endless cellar steps.

To find an echo, listen for the distance, I loose off a shot with my free hand and turn my head for the sound of the bullet coming back. But the ice-sheet fractures instantly below. And out of the splintering mass of the world the white hart flinches into life, jumps from its sleep, hoisting me miles high as it climbs from its knees to its feet. Staggering from the slopes and mountains of its own self, acres of snow avalanche either side of its spine. When it rips back its head to its full height and sets out into the further regions of white, I am far up in the breathless layers of the sky, riding its antlers, lashed to the living horn of the white hart, suspended above a crater of dark, dry blood, between the two black moons of its eyes.

From Nothing to the First of You

Where Nothing wants you, wails it doesn't,
howls you into wretched hugging,
strips you from the sea to merely
sling you back half-stiff half-orphan –

When Nothing cowered and humped in coves
and mapped your mazy plunging progress,
made a boat of bone of fishbird,
wrecked it undershoe and shivered –

Something drew you, drew you on,
set down the silver bobbing throne
on somewhere, cast you cold about it,
something had become expectant –

All your evil, ice and failure,
all your slaughterous fool palaver,
rotten anger, righteous hunger,
death hot, death cold, death in armour
better this than Nothing ever –

And Nothing knows it when it's lonely,
plotting progress of tomorrow's
torment in a vein of envy,
hates you with a smile while sleeping –
shakes that dogging dream of something,
aches all morning of its echoes,
scratches out then out your surname
stuck in a loveheart, loving Nothing.

Planetariumism

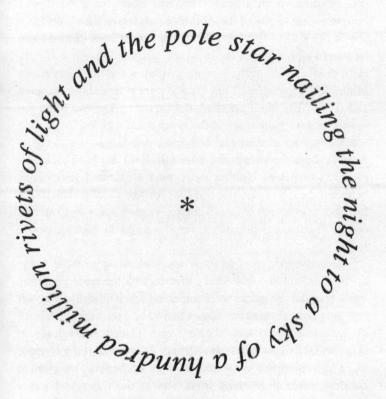

and the pole star nailing the night to a sky of a hundred million rivets of light

*

St Laurence Justinian's Day

Because they were late checking in for flight 052 to Akureyri they were allocated separate seats, Petersson being placed between two members of an aspiring Icelandic death-metal band, and Jamesson next to one of the country's numerous Miss Worlds, or one of her sisters. But even through a fuzz of back-combed and lacquered blond hair (a factor which restricted the view of both men) the scene out of the aeroplane window was an object lesson in physical geography. They passed over a landscape mangled and split by fire, then polished and carved by ice, and when the twenty-seater finally reached the north coast it glided into a wide valley along an alluvial plain, to bank one hundred and eighty degrees above the town at the side of the fjord and head back for a runway which was nothing more than a glorified jetty. They collected their hire car, stopped for provisions in the town (three full circuits in search of an off-licence, vaguely successful) and set out for Myvatn, arriving at their farmhouse on the lakeside before lunch.

The accommodation in itself was something to write home about. The building was Alpine in style, with the rented quarters upstairs under the apex roof, comprising seven or eight rooms off one long central corridor. Shoes had to be removed to preserve the polished floor, and slippery rugs placed strategically at corners and hairpin bends were lethal. At one end of the corridor was a well equipped and spotlessly clean kitchenette, too clean to consider cooking anything in it, and at the other end was a communal living-room, incorporating a wide-screen television that received Icelandic Ceefax on seven channels. To their surprise, Mr Jamesson and Mr Petersson found themselves sharing a room for the first time, despite the absence of any other lodgers for the evening and the availability of four other bedrooms, and questions were asked about snoring and other nocturnal mannerisms.

For a change of scenery and a square meal, they took themselves thirty yards down the street to a large roadhouse, and ate well and cheaply. Jamesson was looking truly expeditionary by this stage of the trip, wearing a length of army webbing around his neck and boasting the beginnings of a shaggy red beard. They wrote a couple of dozen postcards, and sat there most of the afternoon with their notebooks open, occasionally requesting other diners to take photographs of them looking industrious and literary, and selecting records from an imaginary jukebox.

In the evening, they drove four or five miles to the Krafla area, a journey that took them through the space-age pipes and installations of a geothermal energy plant, with columns of brilliant white steam bursting from valves and outlets against an electric-blue sky. On foot, they wandered along a trail that wound its way around a collection of sulphur pools, all gargling and gurgling at boiling point, then followed signposts and arrows towards the lava stream on the other side of the hill. In effect, the lava formed more of a sea or lake, and at the place where they reached it it stood about two yards high, like a charcoal-coloured coral reef, extending for what must have been ten or fifteen miles to the north. Around its edges the liquid rock had cooled and solidified into crazy shapes and sizes, some of them intricate and fragile, others immense, fully formed, already part of the planet. But on the whole the place was still on the move, and it helped to think of it as a living creature, inching its way forward, creeping over the thin soil and blackening everything beneath it. In the 1700s, after one eruption, the lava flowed as far as the lake back at the farmhouse, causing it to boil, then dry up, and to look on it now was to witness something that was far from finished, something that was sleeping it off at the top of the hill, waiting to be woken.

They wandered further into the ash and cinders, feeling the

ground becoming warmer underfoot and with a smell like the smell of scoured wool filling the air, and having passed through a canyon of twisted and torn stone they arrived in a crater or hollow with an altar of smoking rock at its centre, in the shape of an anvil. It was difficult to remember that this was the earth being made, a site of renewal and replacement, and not the scene of some apocalyptic ending or the embers of devastation, which was how it felt. Where all the fires go when they go out. More than that, it felt real and symbolic at the same time, as if it stood for all destruction, marked by the bringing together of elements in their final form, materials and compounds reduced to their lowest natural state, the aftermath of the aftermath, slumbering in an incense of smoke and steam.

On the other side of the hill they visited the area where the Americans had practised the moon landings, and staged a radio dramatisation of the event, starring Mr Petersson as Ground Control, and Mr Jamesson as Neil Armstrong, fluffing his lines again and reporting a low-flying puffin over the Sea of Tranquillity.

A Low God on Krafla

A god will prick the bellies of the clouds
To see what happens, one will set the fire
To melt the place, he knows that happens, one
Will make a fool of blood near where we come from,
But one will make a beeline for Krafla.

Rip bits off and smell them, put them back.
Look it's easy. Crock bits off, they're rotten.
Crumble them, how stuck they are, how broken.
How weird and cheap the earth got at Krafla.
Make a wish on smoke, nobody does that.

This is really ugly. You waltz up
And say it has a sort of grandeur. I know
That's frankly puffinshit. This thing is Krafla.
This soil has never seen us and it's screaming.
Refugee would be the least crap image.

Whatever unreported war threw up this,
Here it is, terranean on Krafla,
Black, fuming, cracking, photogenic, shitey
Grey souvenir for iffy middle children.
Pocket it, think better of it, bin it.

The lowest god you get is king of Krafla.
Go yellow from his stink. He won't show you
His fabulous lagoons so near at hand, though,
And green as heaven. Them you have to look for.
He's not as proud of what was no trouble.

¶

From where we stand
a mountain in heat
lets go

its petticoat of snow,
slips into something
strapless,

backless,
off the shoulder
and below.

Sheep
come off its slopes
with blackened faces,

blistered feet.
Undocked,
one ram

to fifty ewes,
each tail
a lighted fuse.

Tuesday 6th September

'Farmers late with harvest mocked by neighbours this day'

The journey to Dettifoss Waterfall was a three-hour hard drive along a road distinguished only by a smaller gauge of rocks than those to the left and right, and they were accompanied on this leg of the trip by two German backpackers, picked up on a desolate plateau during the first rain in two weeks. They entered the national park of Jokulsargljufur, remarkable as all such places are for the incidence of rope-cordons around interesting or dangerous features, dissuading anyone from imaginative exploration or death. The waterfall itself was more impressive than the guidebooks had predicted, Europe's most powerful in fact, delivering an inconceivable number of gallons of clay-coloured water per second into a long narrow gorge, and causing rainbows at every angle. Surprisingly, there was nothing to stop the two of them crawling up to the edge on their hands and knees and throwing rocks into the abyss, rocks that became nothing immediately, like snowflakes drifting into a blast furnace. After which they followed the course of the river towards the coast, arriving at Vikingvatn Farm mid-afternoon.

The farmhouse was immaculate. The main feature of the living-room was a four-seater burgundy leather settee, which put everything else in its place, and the walls were lined with books, including a three-volume set entitled *The Ornithology of Iceland*, which presumably doubled as a menu. Above the shelves were oil paintings of local scenes, framed maps, and family photographs going back several generations. The curtaining appeared to be Skopos and many of the furnishings were IKEA, though how those things had been acquired and delivered was only to be guessed at. All the floors were polished wood, with more banana-skin rugs at the top of the stairs and next to the bath, and the bathroom was gleaming white ceramic with chrome fittings. They ate with the family after the man of the house had come back from the fields, then sat outside and finished off what was left of the vodka with the help of the two backpackers, tenting it in the corner of the garden. On going back inside for an early night, Mr Petersson and Mr Jamesson agreed how comforting it was to be staying in a house where the television was covered over at night with a heavy cloth, like a budgie cage. After a quick browse through the rest of the schedule, they tipped all their remaining money into a hat and tried to calculate how long it might last. In the morning, the horse-riding had to be skipped because of an early flight from Akureyri, but they did have time to drive to the headland – their furthest point north, ever – and look meaningfully out towards the Arctic.

The Young Recalled

As grasses spider out of ash
    The mortals clear the plain,
The sky is huge and all it has
    It loves to death again,
The locals get the point and shrug
    And slough you like a name,
But the young are parked and clambering out
And breathing deep and have no doubt
    They're brilliantly the same.

They're here as if it started here
    But started yesterday,
They might congratulate you if
    You hike across their way,
Because you couldn't help but turn
    Two queries to one cry.
On lava they will want to know
Exactly where the saplings grow
    In pairs, impossibly.

In bars, on balconies, they smile
    Across the bright remains
Of what they haven't met, they yawn
    Or gossip down the lanes,
Then happen on a bay of light
    That stills them like the lines
That brought them here and burn away
Out to the sky, out to a day
    That isn't there but shines . . .

A figure there recalls the young
    Serenely, as she sips,
With anecdotes and eulogies
    And rumours on red lips,
And nobody is young that day
    Or listens or has hopes,
But, tipsy in a chattering wood,
Each, abandoned to be good,
    Lights cigarettes and copes.

The young, once, on a wilderness,
    Unfrightened, unprepared,
They're driving where the dead got out
    All muffled up, and stared,
Where stone and water radiate
    To hatch a grasping word:
The young have been and left this sound
To grow in all but hopeless ground
But grow in all but hopeless ground
    And prosper, and be heard.

¶

From where we stand
the rivers
are rivers of salmon,

rivers of molten metal,
rivers of earth.
A waterfall waits, looms

on the brink, then trips
a mile-on-mile
production line of mist.

When gale-force streams
seize up
at fifteen below

the hand-drawn coast
in the shape of a duck
or a whale becomes bridged

from beak or tail
to Greenland's toe
by a state of cold.

waterwaterwate r
waterwaterwate r f

```
              f
                  a
          a
                  l
          l
                  l
          l
                  w
          w
                  a
          a
                  t
          t
                  e
          e
                  r
          r
                  f
          f
                  a
          a
                  a
          a
                  a
          a
        l  l
          l  l
            l  l  rerawwetwertawwaetrwatrewaterwaterwate
              lwararatetarweaertarwarterwaterwaterwate
```

St Cloud's Day

Q: When isn't a fjord a fjord? A: When it Ísafjördur. Which was the kind of thing that was passing for humour by the time Mr J and Mr P boarded the delayed flight to that very place in the far north-west, a flight which put the Nemesis ride at Alton Towers into perspective. The pilot had obviously learned his trade on a trawler, given his ability to capitulate to the force of gravity in the space of one second, only to try and escape the Earth's atmosphere the next, and at one stage Petersson would have testified under oath that the wings of the plane were actually flapping. A swelling stream of cups, cans, bottles and fallen luggage flowed up and down the aisle, but after an hour or so of diving and climbing they entered into a gentler descent, leaving behind them the complicated air currents of the interior.

Assuming the danger was over, Petersson raised the blind on his window, only to be mortified by the sight of a valley side no more than twenty feet away, a dark, vertical wall of stone and grass. This picture remained the same for about five minutes, until they flew into a patch of low cloud, and Petersson kept his eyeballs pressed against the glass, thinking that at any second he might be face to face with a golden eagle or a startled mountaineer. Suddenly the plane reared upwards and to the left, as if it were navigating the wall of death, and came back down in the opposite direction. As they emerged from the cloud, Petersson was relieved to see that the view from his window was now mostly air, but a moment later noticed the opposite wall of the valley flashing past the windows on the other side of the plane, even closer this time.

When they finally landed and staggered down the steps, it was possible to see that the aeroplane had needed to turn about inside the canyon of the fjord, which was almost sheer on both sides, and looking closely Petersson thought he could make out grooves and scratches high up on the rock face, caused by the wing-tips of light aircraft. They collected the car which was to be theirs for the remainder of the trip, and spent the night in the Ísafjördur Hotel, watching Iceland go down one–nil to the Swedes on television, with their man Gudni Bergsson having a tidy game in defence.

The Nativity of the Blessed Virgin

Petersson's notebook from the morning of Thursday 8th
September reads as follows:

Up early but couldn't rouse J from his room, so after a
continental breakfast decided to make a quick tour of the town
then return to the hotel for food proper. Ísafjördur can be seen
on foot in an hour, the main settlement being located on a
knuckle of land extending into the water, almost strangling the
fjord into a dam at its narrowest point. The pavements are of
concrete flagstones, a foot and a half square, and the kerbs are
striped or continuously yellow, to discourage or prohibit
parking. The houses are one-, two- or three-storey, all
occupying roughly the same base area, mostly clad with painted
metal, either beaten to the texture of dressed stone or
corrugated. The metal is presumably for the purpose of
preservation with decoration a secondary function, and is, as
House and Garden would put it, an elegant solution to a
problem of practice. The oddest houses are those without
paint, being simply the colour of tin. The predominant colours
are rust, chocolate, mustard, lilac and mint, with doors and
fall-pipes painted in contrasting but complementary shades, all
except the nursery which is pea-green and custard-yellow.

Gardens, where they exist, are bounded by white picket
fencing with decorative iron gates, and many boast a ship's
mast of flagpole to at least the height of the house. The
exterior of every dwelling seems to sport some symbol of hard
work such as a toolbox left open on the path, a pair of leather
gloves resting next to heavy-duty steel-cap boots on the
doorstep, or a boiler-suit hanging from the door handle, giving
the impression of clean and tidy interiors, with families sitting

down to breakfast after two or three hours of industry. The town graveyard is walled, central and kept. All this exists within the two walls of the valley, which seem ready to interlock at any moment. In that respect, the town appears temporary, makeshift, and fortunate.

Mid-morning when they packed the car, consulted the map and traced the intended route with their fingers, following bold red roads that they knew would be nothing more than tyre tracks over stony ground. According to their itinerary, the rest was 'free-range driving' – no one else to speak to, no estimated times of arrival, no deadlines to make. From this point onwards it was due west, until the money or their patience ran out. Jamesson flicked the spherical compass suctioned to the dashboard and watched its dithering green arrow settle towards the mountain in front of them, and Petersson let out the clutch, zeroing the mileometer with his right hand and yanking at the seat-belt with his left, letting the car steer its own way out of the cark park.

Tachograph

West, alongside running water, low gear climbing cinder tracks, around elbow-angles, dropping it down for the revs, driving the bends, taking the view from a passing-place. Over the brow of the first in the range, spot-height to the east, checked and named, through a cutting or pass, eyes to the front, four miles one-in-five downhill, test the brakes. West, sweet-going single track beside a silver-plated lake, metalled at last, slow up for the bridges, narrow gauge, breathe in, nearside and offside mirrors for whiskers, spare inches. West, fallen boulders, road closed unpassable out of season, five ptarmigan up ahead like tea-cosies, hikers, ten miles to travel one, fjords – up to the armpit and out to the fingertip of each, back onto grit, window up, this year's gravel sluiced by rain, pot-holes and pits, bedrock jiggered by frost, hard on the hands on the wheel, hard on the seat. West, half a junction coming up, good use of the map, good trig, incline to highest point, tightrope between two peaks, arête, pig-iron fence, head in the clouds, sweep down into arable land, common fields, fair going over level ground, front-wheel-drive with back end sliding around, shell out for diesel, last chance before Newfoundland. Still west along contour, following earthflow, downthrow, hanging valleys unjugging milk-like melt-water, into neutral with the slope, radio search for World Service, crank up the tape, foothills ahead, kettle-holes up to the hubs, survival shelter high to the left, new view, cover crops holding acres in place, the freight of ourselves carried in oo–scale over epic terrain, floodplain, bays and bights, essential minerals close at hand, noble metals, mantle on top, up and over banks of kame, intermittent rain, hardpan over there swept clean for the landing of planes, square miles of acid rock, homesteads under the bluff, last farm, last light before west, land-breeze picking up, relief, horizon at last of sea unbroken, ledge-

road under the cliffs, headlights on dip, blue-vein lode in the
stones, sunstruck at the coast, free-wheel down out of landscape
numb with after-shock, end of the day, handbrake stop.

Tachographic

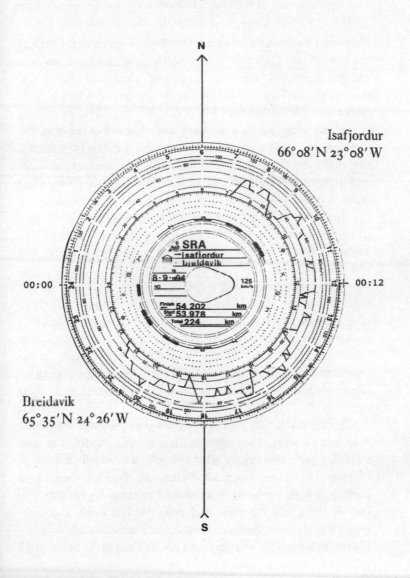

N

Isafjordur
66°08′ N 23°08′ W

00:00

00:12

Breidavik
65°35′ N 24°26′ W

S

¶

I'm sitting way above the farm at Breiðavík, high up at the back of the bay. This is Europe's most westerly point; set out from here and you finish up on the tip of Greenland or the coast of America, the way the Vikings did. It's two in the afternoon. A headland at either side curves out into the ocean, like two arms protecting everything within reach – the track uncoiling out of the hills, the boulders and rocks in the middle distance, the strip of grassland that makes up the apron of the beach, then a mile or so of sand, and then the sea. I can count seven buildings down there, all of them huddled together under the hill for shelter, beginning with the farm itself, a rectangular white bungalow, connected to a three-storey dormitory or bunk-house that looks like a lunatic asylum imported from Eastern Europe. Close by, there are two free-standing wooden sheds, a breeze-block garage, and a long-by-narrow greenhouse with polythene instead of glass, most of it shredded by the wind. And then there's the church. Anywhere else, it probably wouldn't be much more than a pigeon loft or a dovecote, but it does well for itself here, its miniature spire taking whatever elements the Atlantic can throw at it, and the metal cross on top making its point. To the left, a chain-gang of telegraph poles lines up across the hillside, tethered by a single cable.

Glyn's gone wandering off along the coast, around the peninsula, out of sight. I've come inland, turning stones over and following paths that dry up after a couple of hundred yards or go to ground like hunted animals. Behind me there's a steep valley leading to higher ground, but I think I've come far enough. I've lost all sense of perspective and scale this last week, and every time I look over my shoulder towards the horizon I can't decide if it's two miles away or twenty, if it's a walk I can make before dark or not. In and amongst the rocks I can make out a couple of rooks or ravens or crows, scavenging on the ground, and another one just launching itself into mid-air, more like a pair of big black gloves in the shape of a bird than a bird itself, throwing a huge feathered shadow against the side of the hill.

This is the last day and these are the last hours. I should be writing but haven't managed a single word as yet, and I'm hovering with a pen about an inch above a notebook, like the teleprinter in the old sports reports, waiting for the results to come in. On the opposite page, I can just about decipher a few scribbled lines from a piece I once wrote about my sister, and for some reason I'm more interested in that than in all this epic geography going on in the foreground. Maybe I'm just homesick at the moment, but even back at home I don't seem to be able to make anything of anything until it's gone down in history, until it's been transmuted into memory. And the fact that I've written nothing doesn't surprise me, because I'm very slowly coming to the conclusion that all writing comes from the past, from childhood or innocence or naivety, and from loss, lost lives and lives gone by, even the loss of only eight, nine, ten, eleven seconds ago.

Maybe there's some unwritten rule of inversion, to do with distance, a rule that makes the spaceman think of his house, and a room in his house, and a box in that room, and inside that box his most treasured possession, a rule that makes him open the box and look inside it, while orbiting the Earth. It's the rule that brings out the *there and then* from the *here and now*, a rule that I'm very much aware of this precise minute, because this is the sort of place where you rub noses with yourself, catch up with yourself, meet yourself coming back the other way; this is the place where your own face looks back at you, where the days happen in real time, where every moment is simultaneous to itself, synchronised, and where all actions are true to life, unimaginary, right now. This is actuality, the present, and according to the rule I have to get as far away from it as possible.

*

I was always grateful for not being blessed with a brother; being my mum and dad's son was something I never wanted to share with anyone. In my mind's eye I always imagined an older brother as some sort of bully with outsize friends, someone I'd have to contend and compete with, someone whose footsteps I could never follow, especially in his hand-me-down shoes. In the same way, I pictured a younger brother as a kind of precocious runt, borrowing clothes and telling tales in a squealing high-pitched voice, tagging along behind, hanging on to my shirt tails. By the time I was old enough to realise that I'd been spared either or both of those terrors, it started to dawn on me that I had a sister.

We were only young – I don't remember how young exactly – but suddenly it just wasn't right that she should have to share a bedroom with me any more, let alone bunk-beds. Not only was she older than me – a year and a half – but the difference between us seemed to be getting bigger every day, as if she were accelerating out of childhood, repelled by the idea of me or attracted to an image of herself in the not too distant future. She began getting changed under the bedclothes, stopped answering when I whispered to her in the dark, started locking the bathroom door. She wanted the bedroom curtains fully drawn at night so not one ounce of light could interrupt her sleep, and for the little brother who wanted the bedroom door left open and was comforted by the shape of his sister indented in the mattress above him, the eviction notice was about to be served.

At first there was talk of a loft conversion. The house only had two bedrooms, and I wondered what it would be like to climb another set of stairs and to sleep on a different plane above the rest of the family. I worried about lying awake all night staring up at a dormer window, waiting for a mad face to suddenly press itself against the glass. On holiday once, at an overcrowded guest-house, I was led away from my mum and dad and shown to a room in a converted underdrawing, no bigger than an airing cupboard. Birds were roosting in the eaves behind the thin wall, just inches from my face, and eventually I got out of bed and slept on the floor, thinking they might peck through the plaster and attack my eyes and lips with their beaks and claws, their beaks which were tiny scissors, hacking away, their claws which were fish-hooks barbed with spurs and spikes.

But the plan to build a room for me in the attic was either too costly or downright impossible, so it was decided to partition my parents' bedroom, which was L-shaped and seemed to lend itself to being split in half. Of all the rooms in the house, their bedroom was the most magical. Tidy and quiet and holy during the day, full of sunlight which made an altar of my mother's dressing-table and all of its colourful jewels, and powerful at night, as if in their sleep they set up a force-field which spread through the whole house. Passing their room on an evening when they were getting ready to go out was like passing a stage-door, catching glimpses of characters transforming themselves in front of mirrors, choosing from fabulous costumes, helping each other with zips and buttons and laces, loading the air with the spores of powder and hair-spray and scent. The final act, when they eventually presented themselves downstairs, was always my father with his arms down by his side and his chin pointing towards heaven, and my mother adjusting the noose of his tie around his neck, taking it as high and as tight as it would go.

After weeks of delay, weeks of my sister becoming more irritable and secretive, a van arrived carrying long lengths of unseasoned timber and large rectangles of particle-board, to make the dividing wall. My dad's uncle turned up, climbed the step-ladder, and proceeded to divine the position of the joist by tapping the knuckle of his index finger along the ceiling. When the first screw was sunk and it bit into the ancient wooden beam inside the roof-space, he congratulated himself and left us to get on with it. The same day, my dad took a sledge-hammer to a wall and smashed out what was to become the new doorway to their bedroom, filling the house with brick dust and mortar, arriving on the other side like a prisoner of war having tunnelled his way back to England, emerging from the soil with his spade in his hand, expecting a medal. Mum telephoned for a builder. Three or four days later the project was just about finished, apart from a missing board that had to be ordered, which left a hole in the new wall about two feet square, at floor level, and if I crawled through the hole I came out directly underneath my mother's dressing-table, between its two sets of drawers. From their side I probably looked like a dog coming out of a kennel, but to me the hole was the passageway between one world and the next, as close as I'd ever come to finding a new country at the back of the wardrobe. Outside on the landing, the door that had once opened into my parents' room now formed the entrance to a small and private space that was to belong to me and to me only, and for the first time I was in favour of the arrangement. I bought a small metal plate with my name on it, and hammered it to the door.

I was now on the front side of the house rather than the back. Technically speaking, the back was the front and the front was the back, but the house had been polarised long ago by people who could have traced their ancestors back to trees and stones, and that was that. My new room was south-facing and was blasted with sunlight from dawn to dusk whenever cloud cover allowed it, unlike the room I'd been turfed out of, which was permanently in shadow. At a certain time of the year and at a certain time of the day – early summer, mid-morning – sunshine entered the hallway through the keyhole in the front door, and shot a laser beam of light onto the opposite wall at the bottom of the stairs. I once tried to use it as a projector, by holding a slide in front of the keyhole and expecting a picture of my dad with a parrot on his shoulder to appear on the wallpaper across the hallway. But the physics of it was all wrong, and the only things to materialise were the royal blue of his cardigan and the flame-red of the parrot's breast, merging together as a deep, unfocused purple.

The new room also overlooked the whole of the village, which was enclosed on three sides by steep fields rising onto empty moors, and its buildings were cupped in the palm of the valley, cornered almost, with the hillsides bearing down on them three hundred and sixty-five days a year. In the evening, though, the lights from the houses and streets seemed to pool together to make a sort of orange dome, a canopy, as if the village were generating its own atmosphere, its own sky. From my vantage point, about halfway up the valley side, I could see every detail and every movement as it happened, like staring into the magnified workings of a watch. At one stage, I was so mesmerised by the comings and goings in the village at night that as soon as it fell dark I got into bed, turned out the bedroom light and stared out of the window, sometimes for two or three or four hours at a time. It was like gawping endlessly into a planetarium or aquarium – every minute something new came into focus, emerged from the shadows, surfaced from the depths – and the longer I watched, the more I could pick out as my eyes widened to the darkness, a darkness that was punctuated with headlights, brake-lights, street-lights, house-lights, and every other kind of brightness or reflection.

If the moon was out then everything would be edged with silver and grey, and on those nights the view was a scene from a home movie, flickering as clouds passed overhead; or if the sun was taking its time to set then the village became bronzed, sepia-tinted, a ghost of itself from a different time. If it rained the whole picture was glazed and shimmering, and on those nights every car was a small boat, sending out a new ripple across the valley, which had become a harbour. I began to notice patterns, sequences of events that repeated themselves night after night, until I knew what to look for – what incident to expect, at which co-ordinate, and at what hour. In the very middle of the village, high above everything else, the illuminated clock on the Mechanics' Hall became a kind of control tower or centre of operations, as if every action was governed by the fine movements of its cogs and springs, as if the twelve numerals on its face were a kind of zodiac, with all things determined by it, directed by its hands. Like a poor relation somewhere behind me in the darkness, the church clock occasionally attempted to signal the hour, usually at the wrong moment, usually with the wrong number of chimes.

The window itself had become an Advent calendar, with little scenes and episodes and sketches opening up throughout the evening at different points on the glass. But the real reward for all this surveillance came well after midnight, if I could stick it out that long, when my dad arrived home from wherever he'd been and whatever he'd been doing – singing, usually, in a theatre or hall, somewhere in the county. I'd recognise the sound of his car, the pitch of the engine as he tore up the hill at the back in second gear, then watch the arc of the headlights searching a quarter of the sky as he turned the corner, then hear the final clunk of the car door in the yard at the side of the house. In summer, he'd walk out into the garden underneath me, still in his dinner-jacket and white shirt, sometimes to trail a watering-can along a line of flowers or to pick tomatoes in the greenhouse, but mainly just to stand there looking out into the village, smoking, thinking his thoughts, letting the night come to an end. It would have been the easiest thing in the world to tap on the glass, to let him know I'd been watching out for him, waiting for him. But I never did. I stayed silent above him like a star, transfixed, adoring every single thing that he did, every movement that he made, everything he stood for.

The back door opened onto stone flags, then onto a steep and narrow road that somebody once said had been built by the Romans. It sheered away to the right at forty-five degrees, but because it didn't go anywhere of any importance it was always quiet and always safe. On the other side of the road was a grass banking about thirty feet high that completely overshadowed the house, as if facing north didn't make it dark enough in the first place, and even from the upstairs windows it was impossible to see what was above and beyond it. I spent most evenings on my own, kicking a football high up the banking and waiting at the bottom for it to roll back down. The game was to let the ball bounce once on the road, then hoof it up there again, on the volley, and so on, until it came down the slope so quickly that I couldn't control it, or I miscued and sent it spinning off down the road. The steepness of the banking, the speed of the ball and the angle of the road made it an exercise in timing and balance, at which I became a world expert, even if the world could only be measured in terms of the height of the bank, the circumference of the football and the distance I could kick it without falling flat on my back.

When the original football met its end in the clutches of a blackberry bush, I prised the money out of a presentation set of decimalised coins and bought another one. The new ball came flat, deflated, like a shrivelled head, or what I imagined a punctured lung might look like. Sellotaped to it was a tiny metal adaptor, and I took the ball into the cellar and rammed air into it with a bicycle pump until it became hollow and hard. Even bouncing it on the stone floor of the cellar I could tell that the thing was lively, alive even, as if it couldn't wait to work off some of the pressure inside it; and when I walked out of the passageway onto the road and punted it forward, it sailed straight over the top of the banking and was still heading upwards when I lost sight of it. I had no idea what was up there – the top of the bank had been the horizon since the day I was born, and I had visions of the ball being attacked by dogs or stolen by other children, or careering down a hill towards a river and being carried off to sea.

After hauling myself up and over the top, I arrived in a field that was empty and flat, and I could see the football about thirty feet away, its orange forehead standing out above the grass. I was about to walk forward and collect it when I turned sideways and saw the village, laid out beneath me, recognisable but also completely different from this new perspective, this elevation. It struck me now as a map, or a plan, with some lanes radiating from the centre and others spiralling out or encircling the last of the houses. To one side, the main road looked like a dark, slow river of tar, following the lowest contour of the valley. I was so high up I could even see down onto the top of the church tower, where the lightning conductor was lashed to the flagpole, and where a tiny trap-door covered in beaten lead opened out from the belfry. The whole picture was one of roofs and slates and chimneys, more uniform and ordered and comprehensible than the village that existed at street level, like a scale model of itself, every detail perfect. Closer to, I realised I could see straight into the back bedroom of my house, my sister's bedroom as it now was, and the bathroom as well. There were three other houses in the terrace, staggered down the hill, and it puzzled me that their rooms were arranged differently, with different furnishings and fittings, beds in the wrong position, wardrobes up against the wrong wall.

It was getting late in the evening, but when I reached the place where the football was waiting for me, I decided to walk just a little bit further, maybe to the next fence. The field dipped away into a ditch or trench about ten feet deep and the same distance across, and to carry on I had to drop down into it and follow the course of what could once have been a stream. The village had disappeared behind me, gone down below the horizon like the sun, as the ditch led out into a small hollow, where there was a single wall, not connected to anything else, seven or eight courses high in red brick. I jumped over it a couple of times and walked along the top of it, then noticed to the right a thicket of brambles and small trees with a cleared space in the middle. I thought about trying to get in there, but the trees that protected it were frightening, gnarled and knotted together, each one throttling and choking the next, all black and without leaves, strangled with briers and roots. They seemed neither alive nor dead, just a tangle of dislocation and double-jointedness, and they were rotten and damp to touch, and speckled with luminous orange insect eggs. Growing on one of the tree trunks was a great fungus, like a big ear covered with white hair, and when I looked further in I could see other trees sprouting the same things but more hideous and contorted, some like deformed faces of gargoyles, some like kneecaps or fists, others like chunks of meat or tripe, or snails, sucking and clinging to the trees.

I walked on, scrambling over a broken-down gap in a dry-stone wall and into yet another field, which swept upwards to an escarpment on the left. Eight or nine enormous trees were growing out of the slope, elms possibly, that had stretched so high to try and reach the sunlight over the brow of the hill. They were bare, without limbs or branches apart from a few withered tentacles at the very top, unclimbable, and each in its own space, at a similar distance from the next.

I was just coming out from between the trees, over the ridge of the escarpment, when I had to stop. In front of me, only an arm's length away and level with my face, was the body of a huge animal, a cow, massive and still, lying on its side. I was too close, close enough to see the patterns in its hide – not just the colours but the nap of the hairs, twisted and matted with dirt, stained with grass, as well as the veins in its skin where the hide was threadbare or bald, and the knuckles of its backbone and the struts of its ribs, and the swags of flesh, rolls of it, hardening around its shoulders and neck. I could have reached out and touched it, but that was the last thing I wanted to do – I didn't even want to breathe the air around it, and I pulled my jumper up over my mouth as a kind of mask. More than anything else, though, was its sheer size, gigantic, tons of it, and what kept me silent and frozen there was the thought that it might suddenly jolt back to life, that it might haul itself to its full height in front of me, making the ground shudder, or lash out with its legs.

The safe course would have been to retreat, to backtrack quietly down the slope, but I found myself inching around towards its front, as if its face might hold an answer or a clue, or some expression of sleep or rest or peacefulness that I might recognise. But its eyes were missing, leaving two dark holes where the skin was collapsing over the sockets, and its mouth was open, the lips pulled back showing off the arrangement of its teeth and its tongue, like the stump of an arm. I stood there for ten minutes or more, and must have looked like a skull and cross-bones, with my arms folded over my chest, hugging my shoulders, and my face floating somewhere above them, shocked and colourless.

Eventually, I sidled along the escarpment and climbed over the ridge at a different place. It was brighter there, coming out into what was left of the light, out from the shadow of the slope and away from the presence of the trees. I ran on ahead, wanting to get into open ground and be out of range of the cow, but it had bothered me, and I kept wondering if anyone knew about it, whether it was waiting to be collected, or if it had been killed. I'd never known death like that before – close by, immense, unexpected. And silent as well, private, just for me. As if the body had been lying there in wait.

I was getting higher, into an area that was unwalled and unfenced, a sort of no-man's-land between where the fields ended and the moors began. I arrived on the side of what I thought was a small hill, and its contours took me around to the left. Down in the bottom, to my right, was a stream with what looked to be a path running alongside. Thinking that the path was a good place to be – somewhere that other people had been – I began dropping down towards it, but suddenly caught sight of another cow, at the side of the stream, with its legs sticking out above it, its neck twisted backwards and its head in the water. I stayed on the side of the hill, stumbling along as it became steeper, curving around, and never being able to see more than about twenty or thirty yards ahead. Following the line of the stream with my eyes, and finally rounding the shoulder of the hill, I looked up, and couldn't take another step forward. In front of me was a dead-end, the head of the valley, a wall of darkness, as if I was stood at the mouth of an enormous cave. The horizon seemed to be miles above me, almost indistinguishable from the black sky that formed a kind of roof, and I had to kneel down and hold on to the grass. The sides of the valley were covered in stones and boulders that seemed to have been hurled down from the top, and the slopes were so severe – almost vertical – that I couldn't understand why the stones hadn't fallen all the way down into the stream at the bottom. I looked back for some sense of where I was, some reminder of the way I'd come, but the valley had folded in behind me. I decided to stand up and move forward a yard or so, just to try and get my bearings and my balance, but when I did the horizon raised itself up and lunged forward, threatening to extend all the way overhead.

This was as far as I could go. I shuffled backwards, slowly, then stood again and began to walk in the opposite direction. I didn't run; I knew not to run from danger, and I didn't want the force and power of the valley to be chasing me along the hillside, didn't want to start an avalanche, didn't want to be the focus of any more attention. I followed the side of the hill until the valley opened up to let me out, came off the moor towards the escarpment and dropped through the elm trees, well away from the cow. I crossed the field, steering clear of the tangled wood, and saw the small red-brick wall up ahead. Not being able to hold back any longer, I broke into a sprint and hurdled the wall, and as I raced up the ditch towards the last field I could feel the whole volume of the empty valley over my shoulder, its capacity, as if I were trying to outrun the water from a great dam that had burst its banks, or a tidal wave.

I could see the village now, and the chimney of the house. I scooped up the football without stopping, like someone snatching a baby out of harm's way, slithered down the banking, crossed the road and went into the house. My mother was ironing in the kitchen, in the dark, and when I turned on the light we stood there, her with the iron in her hand, me with the football, staring at each other.

Once I'd let some air out of the ball, a couple of weeks later, I began playing the game again, but now I'd conquered the banking I was more interested in hoofing the thing over the horizon and chasing it up there, just so I could sit and watch the world going round. Mostly, I'd be on the look-out for my mum coming home, in the days before I was old enough to be trusted with a door key (the back door – the only thing that ever came in through the front door was that laser beam of sunlight in the summer). She'd begin her journey as a small dot, recognisable by the colour of her coat or her black hair, crossing the road from one shop to another, or chatting with somebody else on the pavement. Sometimes I'd follow her movements for about half an hour, from the butcher's to the post office, from the post office to the greengrocer's, then to the chemist's, only to realise that I'd been tracking the wrong person – at which point I'd look around frantically, scanning every road and junction until I caught sight of her wandering towards me with a bag full of bread or vegetables in each hand. By the time she'd reached the bottom of the road, about three or four hundred yards below me, she'd be coming into focus, unmistakable, and growing bigger and more real with every step. Finally, I could make out the expression on her face, and she'd glance up and see me, waiting like a cat in the grass at the top of the banking, and smile. She couldn't call out because she was usually out of breath by then, and she couldn't wave because her arms were loaded down with shopping.

My mother wasn't born in the village, she was from somewhere else, somewhere different, eight or nine miles away. Her own mother had come to Yorkshire from Cheshire, sent away to relatives when she was small. She was the youngest of nine, the last straw. She still lived in the house where my mum had grown up, but it came as a big surprise to me when I finally realised that my grandma was actually my mum's mum – that she'd actually given birth to her. Before that I'd just thought of her as one of the family, without any specific connection, simply a relative.

My grandma was a tiny woman who seemed to get smaller and smaller as I grew up. She kept having to have her rings altered so they didn't fall off her fingers, kept having to drop down a size in dresses and shoes, stand on more and more boxes to peg the washing out on the line or reach the pots and pans in the cupboard. Or so I imagined. She had wonderful clear skin on her hands and her face, translucent almost, which I thought was the result of the harsh-smelling soap she kept in her bathroom. She she knew all the names of the flowers and trees, and how to spell them, and what they meant.

One morning we had a phone call to say that she'd been lying on the kitchen floor all night, calling out and banging on the wall, desperate to make the next-door neighbour hear her, and when we arrived at the hospital one side of her face was lifeless and fixed, and the other side was tearful and afraid. And she was even smaller, her feet reaching no further than halfway down the bed, her voice like the voice of a child in another room, trying to tell us something, her two miniature slippers parked next to each other under the bedside table, like toy cars. Every time we visited she was a little bit smaller, a little further away, and I'd brush her hair, stroke the skin on her face, pare her nails and let her good hand curl into a fist around my finger. She died at Christmas. Before the funeral service they asked me if I wanted to go into the room to see her for one last time, but I didn't need to. I could already picture her, lying like a baby in a cot, like a doll in a shoe box, asleep on a bed of cotton wool with a hankie for a blanket and a glove for a pillow, all of her face unlocked and at peace with itself.

My sister was eighteen months old when I was born. My family had lived in a different house up until then, and sometimes I come across packets of photographs that predate me, black and white snaps of my mother and father with their only child – a bouncing, blonde daughter – standing there in unfamiliar rooms, like distant relatives. When we were small, my sister always had the upper hand. We fought a lot, and I lost a lot. I took up judo to frighten or impress her, but she just laughed at me, dancing around in front of her in my little outfit, a sort of kimono-cum-smoking jacket made out of woven asbestos. Finally, though, during one bout, I punched her with my fist and gave her a black eye, and there and then the fighting stopped. From that point onwards, we had to find some other form of communication. Oddly enough, every one of my friends had an older sister, so we belonged to a fraternity that knew what it meant to wear a girl's white blouse for cricket practice and to wait patiently outside the bathroom door for an hour twice a day, and we were united by it.

At secondary school she didn't mind being spotted with me, and after my voice had broken I was allowed to be heard as well as seen. Like all younger brothers I was smitten by her friends, who I thought of as celebrities and super-models, and I felt like a ball-boy in the ladies' locker-room at Wimbledon when they invaded the house at weekends, grooming each other for hours at a time. Pretty soon she was setting off on Saturday nights when I was just coming back from the woods with a bag full of conkers, and arriving home on Sunday mornings when I was just getting out of bed to do a paper-round. She'd given up smoking before I knew she'd started, then one day she was gone, away to college at the other end of the country, and the house was a cemetery. I thought about moving back into the bedroom where I'd started out from, but it was a shrine now, left the way she wanted it, not to be desecrated under any circumstances.

Two years ago she had a baby, a little girl, and the shape of the family changed overnight. What before had been a complicated network of ties, connections and couplings, like a cat's-cradle with its vectors and junctions, became a simple formation with the baby at the centre, the hub, and all spokes leading out from her. I remember my dad's face at the hospital, an unfathomable picture of glory and relief and bewilderment. She's having another baby, next summer, and somewhere deep down I can't help thinking of it as a boy, a brother.

I'm driving over the moor. It's evening, the sun going down in the rear-view mirror, dusk beginning to happen up ahead. The landscape suddenly opens up as I know it will, a flight of reservoirs damming the valley to the right, a set of quarries stepping down from the hillside in front of me, a matrix of steep fields and half-hearted dry-stone walls to the left, and down in the very bottom, the village, anchored into the bedrock, holding everything else in place. On the fringe of the moor there's a square of emerald green, a flag of perfectly ironed lawn, the most unlikely bowling-green in the country, and probably the highest. I stop the car and watch a man rolling out four woods from one corner of the green to another, diagonally, then back again, walking behind the last bowl as it trundles towards the jack, ushering it into the winning position, then shepherding them all together with his feet and setting them off again, slow, heavy, easy, curling away from him, pulling up short of the gutter, forming a new constellation where they come to rest.

It's my dad. He's out there on his own, full of himself, miles away. This is his patch. High above him are the shallow black tarns he discovered as a boy, the kingdom of dark, silent water that no one else seemed to have heard of. To one side of him is the golf course – fairways and greens under siege from bulrush and tussock grass – where he scattered his uncle's ashes, whether the committee approved of it or not. Behind him, the cricket pitch, where he tore in from the boundary and uprooted the stumps of every batsman in the league, summer after summer after summer. And just out of sight, the steep ravine where he hid one day, when half the village was out looking for him. He took me there once, to show me the place, but couldn't find it. I thought he'd be disappointed, defeated, but he put his hands on my shoulders and told me what it proved – that whoever hid there would never be discovered.

This is his place, his element. Every gate, corner, path, field, wall, stream, every point on the compass is primed, charged with some event from the past; and here he is at the centre of it all, at its heart, conducting it, touching off memory after memory, commemorating himself, comforted by it, but at the same time longing for it all, every second of it, all over again. I'm late, but I wait another minute, watch him roll out the woods one more time, steer them into the opposite corner of the green, stop to light up and flick the matchstick away with his free hand, then set out after them, to collect them and begin.

*

I'm late, but I wait another minute before wandering back down the hillside to the farm. The tide's out – miles out – but it's on the turn, and I can see the Atlantic Ocean dealing shallow waves onto the shore, each wave scurrying inland and laying down a silvery-white line at its furthest point, along its leading edge, before draining back to sea. In the middle of the bay I can see Glyn, heading this way, a long thin shadow stretching out in front of him, towards me. He's strolling back from the beach with his trousers rolled up above his knees, wearing a bright-red T-shirt and a shoe on each of his hands, leaving a trail of footprints behind him, looking for all the world like a man just arriving here from a long walk across the water.

Harald and the Lonely Hearts

ACT III

Nervous in the wings, the NORTHERN LIGHTS *prepare to shine.*

Song of the Northern Lights

not a song no
> no such thing no
>> north is no where
> light is we oh

what arise is
> rage of rain bow
>> have to hinge it
> from a prayer oh

cold we mean is
> all we come to
>> nail up high where
> how we beg to

sad to see your
> eyes so royally
>> so enrapt oh
> seeing we so

weep to learn oh
> we are heaven
>> if we are heaven oh
>>> where go we oh

(Down on the plain, the LONELY HEARTS *have been dancing for several days, drinking Hoskuld's coffee and falling for him. Only* INGE, MAGNUS *and* KARINA *have still to drink.*)

Song of the Lonely Hearts (*reprise*)

Call us the swingers and call us the sinners,
Call us the wags and the wits and the winners,
Here's where we reign in the palm of the plain,
A million litres of happiness in us!

INGE

Lonely I am in the palm of the plain
I wish I could slouch in the city again
For that was my way and I'm missing the day
And I'm missing my dog and my dad and my lane.

Call us the swingers and call us the sinners,
Call us the wags and the wits and the winners,
Here's where we stand in the lie of the land,
A million litres of holiness in us!

MAGNUS

Homesick I am in the lie of the land
I wish this was something officially planned
For that's who we are and I'm missing my ma
And I don't think a lot of this Lebanese brand.

Call us the swingers and call us the sinners,
Call us the wags and the wits and the winners,
Here's where we lust at the rim of the crust
A million litres of brilliance in us!

My hope is all dust at the rim of the crust
I wish I had someone to trouble and trust
For he was my beau and I'm missing him so
Though he never knew either. Somebody must.

Call us the swingers and call us the sinners,
Call us the wags and the wits and the winners,
Here's where we're stuck by a rock and a rock,
And a million litres of liberty in us!

HOSKULD

And now, my friends, what a time for a brew,
Now no one is lonely and everyone knows
That Hoskuld's the one with the coffee for you,
The love from the tip of your nod to your toes!

LONELY HEARTS

No one is lonely and everyone knows
The love from the tip of your nod to your toes!

INGE

Lonely I am.

MAGNUS

Homesick I am.

KARINA

Hope is all dust. Somebody must.

HOSKULD

Beauty is me and my flat on the plain,
Where they dance on the bones of the great Althing,
They'll never see Valur play soccer again,
Read Sjön or read Bragi or hear Björk sing!

We dance on the bones of the great Althing,
See Hoskuld, read Hoskuld, hear Hoskuld sing!

INGE

Lonely I am.

MAGNUS

Homesick I am.

KARINA

Hope is all dust. Somebody must.

HOSKULD

I had an idea and it's dearer than blood is,
Look how they sway to it, love how they rear,
Love is the spirit that Hoskuld embodies,
Hoskuld is Lord over Thingvellir!

LONELY HEARTS

Look how we sway to it, love how we rear,
Hoskuld is Lord over Thingvellir!

(*Suddenly the* NORTHERN LIGHTS *appear above the plain, rippling their beautiful colours.*)

Song of the Northern Lights (*reprise*)

> not a song no
>   no such thing no
>   north is no where
>   light is we oh

(HARALD, *alone in a valley, sees the lights, and climbs up the ridge.*)

HARALD

I say, that's something I've seen before,
But I can't say I've ever looked all that closely.
Makes me feel small, I must say, and what's more,
It occurs to me I'm an idiot, mostly.

(HARALD *has not noticed the* LONELY HEARTS *dancing around a great fire on Thingvellir, because the Northern Lights are so bright tonight, but his handsome profile can be seen by everyone.*)

KARINA

It's Harald, how lovely he seems up there!
There's blue in his arms and green in his hair!

MAGNUS

Harald, we're down here, we're sad and we're cold!

INGE

Our friends have gone crazy, we all feel old!

(*Gradually, the* LONELY HEARTS *recognise* HARALD *and start to move towards him, making their way up the ridge.*)

LONELY HEARTS

Call us the lonely hearts, call us the boozers,
Call us the louts and the liggers and losers,
This is our friend we forgot in our trance,
Sing Up with our friendship, and down with the dance!

HOSKULD

What about coffee, what about me,
What does he have that you can't have here?

LONELY HEARTS

No answer, no answer, it just has to be,
Don't hold us to reason what we hold dear.

KARINA

We're blessed by the light.

MAGNUS

We're blessed in the past.

INGE

We're still in the silence.

POETS

(We're still in the cast.)

HERMANN

We're walking home to Old Reykjavík.

GUDRUN

Where we're free to be lonely!

KRISTJAN

And frequently sick.

LONELY HEARTS

Call us the louts and the liggers and losers,
Call us the wags and the wits and the winners,
Call us the lonely hearts, call us the boozers,
A million litres of Iceland in us!

(HARALD *leads the* LONELY HEARTS *back to Reykjavík, leaving* HOSKULD *alone on Thingvellir.*)
(*It is now the early hours of Saturday morning. The* LONELY HEARTS *decide to stand around in the streets for a while, just like old times.*)
(*Suddenly,* HARALD *and* KARINA *break into a song.*)

Chorus of a Happy Couple

Once, we're saying, once go home.
  Once be just together.
Once, we're saying, then we'll live
The same way that we always live
  With everyone for ever.

Soon, we're saying, soon again.
  Again, and just we two.
Soon, we're saying, then we'll live
The same way that we always live
  With these and those and you.

Roll after me, my lovely one,
  Pursue me to the end.
We murmur here with everything
We'll ever need, and everything
  We'd murder to defend.

Time, we're saying, time for this,
  More time than there can be.
Time, we're saying, then we'll meet
The same ones that we'll always meet
  Down by the dogged sea.

(HARALD *and* KARINA *go home together.*)
(*The* LONELY HEARTS *remain on the streets of Reykjavík, where you can see them to this day, before first light on Saturday morning.*)

  The bars will be open, with room in the clubs
  A million of us will go to the pubs
  A million of us could not care more
  That this is our life and here's what it's for!

EPILOGUE

The side of the smouldering volcano Krafla. GLOTA *the troll is sitting*
with SHRUGGA, STURRA *and* DROPPA.

STURRA
You messed it all up. He was almost gone.

GLOTA
I blew it, I know.

STURRA
But I'm not one to gloat.

GLOTA
I blew it, it's true.

SHRUGGA
Let's forget it, move on,
Who cares, anyway. It was fun on that boat.

DROPPA
It could have been Faustus, Midas, Macbeth.
(I was in on all those.) But *you* had to be kind.
You couldn't allow a theatrical death.

STURRA
You let him stand there with the fireworks behind.
Now he's all *happy*, you know? That stuff?

GLOTA
I know it, I blew it.

DROPPA
I've had enough.
I've work with the House of Windsor. PR.
(I'm thick with that lot.)

STURRA

Then you should go far.

(DROPPA *changes into a BBC newsreader and glides away.*)

STURRA

I'm out of here too. I've a job in LA.

GLOTA

What?

STURRA

Oh some trial.

GLOTA

They don't need you.

STURRA

I'll say.

(STURRA *changes into an LAPD officer and screeches away, sirens blaring.*)

GLOTA

You leaving me too?

SHRUGGA

No idea. Can't decide.

GLOTA

Looks like this chap wants to give you a ride.

(*A helicopter lands on the volcano.* SHRUGGA *changes into a general with a light-blue beret and gets in. The helicopter flies away.*)

GLOTA

Easy come, easy go. Not the worst of all work.
You get to meet women, you travel, you learn.

You walk in the sun and you sleep in the murk,
Like everyone really. You takes your turn. See . . .

(GLOTA *changes back into* HOSKULD.)

HOSKULD

Though you are my brother, you miss so much.
It passes you by in the breath behind you.
And if you don't try to, how can you touch?
And if you don't touch us, how will we find you?

Finale

The LONELY HEARTS (in central Reykjavík)

Here you can find us till Reykjavík Town
Is Totally Tropical, here we will stand
Till Snæfell snorts and comes crumbling down
And our hair goes black and our faces brown
And Vatnajökull is turned to sand!
Here will we stand!

HARALD and KARINA (in bed)

Here you can find us till here is cold
And beds are history, here we will lie
Till all of you lose your balances, rolled
In rings of a summer of spiralling gold
And the I in Iceland is only I!
Here will we lie!

The POETS (in this book)

Here you can find us till Hertfordshire
Is a Yorkshire Riding, here we will sit
Till the usual fuss with the ice or fire

Till a Tory is sorry he's been a liar
Till the Beatles form and the Stones split
Here will we sit!

The TROLLS (on the Internet)

Here you can find us till left meets right
And elephants vote for it, here we will play
Till the red sun rises to his full height
And exonerates day and eviscerates night
And Iceland sags like a first soufflé
Here will we play!

ALL TOGETHER (now)

Here you can find us, we do hope you will,
We're sorry it's pricey, it's worth it though.
Fly, or you'll get most emphatically ill,
You want to eat puffin, you eat your fill,
Thick socks, a Minolta, and loads of dough.
Just so you know.

The ENTIRE CAST *stand still, drinking, to the tune of 'The Modern Things' by Björk, until the* NORTHERN LIGHTS *bring down their*

CURTAIN

Breiðavík Farm

Forty-eight Hours at the End of the Land

I

Iceland, day, and our holiday end here,
West as Europe in our world can be,
World in whose light sleep these lonely islands
Tiptoe in and out of history
    Clandestine and sincere
As children or the old through a mother's silence.

Who finds in a lava cave white bones and pearls
Was sure to do: they're set down in the Book.
The story drapes around the fact like fleece,
Concealing nothing if you tug and look,
    And then the pool upswirls,
The mountaintop collapses from its peace,

Shovels its treasure live into the sea
Still smarting, and the air is shorn of birds.
Now life, distressed and disassured, must enter
Into the wrung and riddled hill with words,
    And sink its memory,
Toughen like a story must through winter.

So, neither long ago nor yesterday
But both and always both, the wild who sail
By flocks and stars and temperatures come back
Fit for it, strong, constant as a tale,
    And stumble into day,
Hauling along humanity like slack,

And start out once again for the streamed cave
To hide their few dear pearls from the high ogres.
Around this drones the unpersuaded weather,
Repeating its one proverb about Progress
　　While, logically brave,
These folk, who learn alone, set off together.

II SONG OF HOW TO
(for Simon)

How to pass a day as far
From everything we left and like
As Weldon Kees is from his car
Or T. E. Lawrence from his bike?
As *Voyager* from seeing home,
As Moscow from those Chekhov sisters,
Ends of roads from Rome from Rome
Or us from each who ever kissed us?

How to pass a day as far
From everything we left and do
As Weldon Kees is from his car,
The Flying Dutchman from his crew?
As Zeno's arrow from the mark,
As Halley from its final lap,
As Oncomouse from Noah's Ark,
Or PH from our Iceland map.

How to pass a day as far
From everything we left and rate
As Weldon Kees is from his car
Or Britain from its Welfare State?
As Tipperary is from here,
As miles to go from any sleep,

As what we hope from what we hear,
As what we swear from what we keep.

How to pass a day as far
From everything we left and own
As Weldon Kees is from his car
Or Crusoe from his ansaphone?
As Orpheus from his desire,
As Romeo from Juliet's,
As gyres from every previous gyre,
As corpses from outstanding debts.

How to pass a day as far
From everything we left and miss
As Weldon Kees is from his car,
As wedding days from wedded bliss?
As Eldorado from the eye,
As nectar from the tongue and nose,
As piglets from the evening sky
As roses from the name of rose.

How to pass a day as far
From everything we know and love
As Weldon Kees is from his car
Or everything is from enough?
As everything is from enough,
As wanting is from having to,
As having is from what we love,
As loving is from how we do.

III

West as it was, tired as we were, this Bay
Surprised us with its gentleness, its sea

Serene and blue, its sand the shade of any
Decent childhood beach, and the white sky sunny.

Initialling the shallows with bare feet,
We waded out into the Arctic, let
The water warm a little, for the sake
Of all old holidays, then, end of joke,

Freeze us out like sisters. What we thought
Was yes a whale! was of course a fishing boat,
Pausing and sailing on, and the exotic birds
Were only seagulls. Brits, in other words.

No lava, no lagoons or crater-lips,
No trolls or torrents, storm-deriding ships,
Volcanoes, Vikings, midnight sun or moon:
Us, at the end too soon and none too soon.

Tired as we were, west as it was, this Bay
Surprised us with the warmth and company
Of some we have forever lost. We went
On sand and gravel out to the utmost point

Of western cliffs. We swayed again from harm.
Of all we have to leave, to leave this farm
Was easiest, or hardest to resist,
To spring at dawn from this so patient west.

Last fancy. That the body of this land,
Light sleeper with, beloved in its hand,
Its poets, felt two more – or one on all fours –
And opened in the shoreline of its snores

This smiling creek, this blue familiar sight
For English boys to meet in the fixed light
Of a happiness, but to tell the ones they love:
This you can have, for the last time, this you can have.

174

Listen Here

It will not be got
from the kernel of rock
where a seismograph samples the murmur of stone,
bugging the pulse where quakes assemble
in swarms and drones.

It will not be caught
in the berth of a boat as it trawls.
Marine life idles in absolute time to starboard and port,
the mid-Atlantic splits its stitches
and the blue whale yawns.

It will not be farmed
in the far of the ground. There,
the wind goes out of its way for somewhere to sound,
unloading the scream of the sea
on the shell of the ear.

It will not be traced
to the deep down of a cave,
where a word on the loose is a bird in a box, a black box;
water clocks the midnight days
in slow, synthesised drops.

It will not be told
by the wide open road.
Chippings tune the forks and spokes of mountain bikes
or station-wagons tread and hold
in four-wheel drive.

It will not be bought
for the price of a long walk
above cliffs. Sea-birds needle the air with their beaks,
come close with scraps of talk,
snatches of speech.

It will not be clinched
with equipment, will not be tricked
by holding a microphone out to the air, the water or land
and recording the cracks and clicks
of bones in the hand.

It will not be had,
or fixed. Made of finer stuff,
to find it is to let it come to mind, then bluff,
or lie, or think, or wish.
Now hear this.